Still Laughing
Stories from an Extraordinary Friendship

LUCI RECORD AND **ALYCE HENNELLY**

Still Laughing, published October, 2023
Editorial and proofreading services: Cath Lauria; Katie Barger
Interior layout and cover design: Howard Johnson
Photo Credits: Author photos owned by the authors.
Front cover art: *2 women with coffee*, image by Freepik
Interior artwork (chapter/part openers): *Leafy Branches*, designed by Sketchepedia/Freepik

 SDP Publishing

Published by SDP Publishing, an imprint of SDP Publishing Solutions, LLC.

All rights reserved. No part of the material protected by this copyright notice may be reproduced or utilized in any form or by any means, electronic or mechanical, including photocopying, recording, or by any information storage and retrieval system, without written permission from the copyright owner.

To protect the privacy of certain individuals, names and identifying details have been changed.

To obtain permission(s) to use material from this work, please submit an email request with subject line: SDP Publishing Permissions Department.

Email: info@SDPPublishing.com.

ISBN-13 (paperback): 979-8-9882715-7-4

Library of Congress Control Number: 2023916437

Copyright © 2023, Luci Record and Alyce Hennelly

Printed in the United States of America

Table of Contents

Forward 7
You're Writing What? 7
Introduction 9
    The Cast of Characters 9
    Won't You Be My Neighbor? 9

PART I   The Frazzle Phase: Keeping One Step Ahead of the Katydid Lane Kids 17

CHAPTER
1   Westward Ho to Ohio With Seven Children Twelve and Under 19
2   School Daze 25
3   Slippery Slope 29
4   The Kids, the Camp, and the Cove 34
5   Rocking the Block 38
6   Bonnie and Clyde Come to Katydid 41
7   Christmas Innocence Lost 45
8   Bumps, Bruises, and Emergency Trips 47
9   The Wide, Wide World of Sports 52
10   Smitty's Bog and the Sand Pit 55
11   Bobo 59
12   Little Women, Big Dreams 62

PART II   The Improvement Phase: Tune-Up Time for Mind, Body, and Soul 71

CHAPTER
13   Battling Time and Gravity 73
14   Let's Get Physical 77
15   Teaching Old Dogs New Tricks 88

PART III   The Project Phase: Getting Crafty 93

CHAPTER
16   Pins and Needles and Other Handiwork 95
17   It's For the Birds 106

PART IV	**The Financial Phase: A Gal's Got to Make a Living**..109	
CHAPTER	18	The Pastry Cart 111
	19	Career Girls in the Real World................................ 116
	20	High Rollers and Low Expectations........................ 123

PART V	**The Celebration Phase: Girls Just Want to Have Fun**.. 125	
CHAPTER	21	Ghosts and Goblins on Katydid 127
	22	Progressive Dinners 129
	23	Office Christmas Parties 131
	24	Happy Holidays 136

PART VI	**The Traveling Phase: Cars, Trains, and Planes**... 143	
CHAPTER	25	High Teas 145
	26	Touring Houses and Museums................................ 152
	27	Making Merry in Magog 162
	28	Ooh La La 168

PART VII	**The Shop 'Til You Drop Phase**......................... 175	
CHAPTER	29	Bargain Shopping and Thrifting 177
	30	Thank God for GPS 180
	31	Car Calamities... 182

	Epilogue 187
	Acknowledgments 188
	About the Authors 189

Dedication

*To our husbands and our children,
who have always brought love and
joy to our lives.*

Forward

You're Writing What?

Alyce Hennelly and Luci Record are neither rich nor famous. Their endeavors are not particularly heroic, nor their trials and tribulations epic. Their stories are those of two ordinary women living ordinary lives with their families in a little hamlet south of Boston called Hanson, Massachusetts. Why did they want to share their lives with others?

At first, they planned to write a memoir of their years shared on Katydid Lane for their children. However, through the many hours of writing and compiling the stories of both the children's and their adventures, they have come to appreciate that lasting memories are forged in simple, ordinary experiences with family and friends. Through writing, they discovered more about themselves and the power that friendship and community have to enrich lives.

How does the chance meeting of two neighbors lead to a friendship that has lasted over fifty years? The one constant throughout the years has been laughter. Sometimes that laughter is mixed with tears, and sometimes it is uncontrollable, but it is the filter through which they view life's experiences.

Laughter alone does not define their relationship. Proximity, shared common interests, a love of learning, and an intellectual curiosity are components of friendship, but their relationship is built on a foundation of trust and respect. Though they may hold differing views on some issues, they respect each other's opinions. Over the years, that trust has allowed each woman to push the boundaries of their individual comfort zones and accept new challenges.

While this book is a keepsake for their children to help them reminiscence about their childhood adventures, it also enables their grandchildren to see that their parents and grandparents were indeed young once, with the same fears and emotions, loves, and losses they may experience. Perhaps these stories have a broader appeal as well. They reveal a willingness to accept challenges, to never give up, to cherish and nurture friendships, and to always remember to laugh.

Oh, the joy of laughter.

Introduction

The Cast of Characters

Main Characters:

The Hennellys: Alyce and Ron with Lauren, Deedee, Karen, Allison, and Jill

The Records: Luci and Jim with Jimmy, Steve, and Lauren-Kate

The Neighbors in Order of Appearance:

The Kings: Pete and Rollene with Johnny, Donny, and Greg

The Landrys: Patrick and Peggy

The Swensons: Brad and Joan with Abby

The Gills: Buddy and Maggie with Maura and Blair

The Madisons: Bob and Brenda with Sally and Teddy

The Monteiros: José with Manny and Juan

The Sheas: Son Joey and daughter Amy

The Andersons: Son Sean

Won't You Be My Neighbor?

House hunting is both exciting and terrifying for young buyers. Which town shall they choose? Urban or rural? New house or fixer-upper? Can they afford it? What will the commute be like? Do they need two cars? Is it a safe neighborhood? How is the school system? Will the children be happy there? What are the taxes? What if there are multiple offers? How high do they go?

So many decisions leave young buyers with more questions than answers. Those decisions have a profound effect on a family, especially if you are two stay-at-home mothers with toddlers, commuter husbands, and few resources. The further you were from Boston, the lower the home prices, but the longer the commute. How high would their budgets allow?

Hanson offered much to young buyers in the 70s. First, its rural location away from congested areas was calming and allowed homeowners to enjoy minimum ¾-acre lots. There was plenty of room for backyard sporting events, grills, and swing sets galore. Low taxes, multiple ponds, cranberry bogs, and natural beauty made it a perfect choice. The picturesque new development of Katydid Lane abutted cranberry bogs on one side and Cranberry Cove on the other side.

The Cove, as it was called, was the town beach and a walking path away from the homes. Numerous cabins dotted its many acres. On the other side, the working bog offered myriad examples of natural beauty in all seasons, especially during harvest time when the red berries were water harvested.

Contrary to popular belief, the street was not named for the typically green, long-horned grasshopper called the katydid. The true story is that the family who owned the entire parcel of land gave a lot to their oldest son, who had five children—four older boys and one younger girl. The four rambunctious boys were often mischievous. Whenever the mother shouted, "Who did that?" the boys exclaimed in unison, "Katy did." Thus, Katydid got its name.

At that time in Brockton, Alyce and Ron Hennelly were outgrowing their small home. One morning, while daughters Lauren (five) and Deedee (four) played with dolls in their room, Alyce, noticeably pregnant, waddled to the backyard clothesline to hang her second load of clothes that morning. She waved to Rollene, her next-door neighbor, who was planting flowers in her garden. Rollene brushed the dirt off her knees and went toward Alyce.

After they exchanged casual banter, Rollene added, "Hey, Alyce, I just talked to my cousin. She's really up on real estate. She said Crowley's building a new development in Hanson. It'll be closer to Pete's work, and he wants to buy a lot there. It's right off Route 58. The lots are big too. My three boys really need more room to play. You and Ron should look into it."

"That's good news for you," agreed Alyce. "Good luck."

The seed planted by Rollene grew exponentially. By the time Ron came home from work, Alyce had already calculated the pros and cons and deduced that this might be the perfect move for them too. It didn't take much convincing, and soon both the Kings and the Hennellys moved into their new homes on Katydid in 1970. Alyce almost outgrew the new house with the later births of two more daughters, Allison and Jill.

Alyce met her new next-door neighbors, the Landrys, in a most unexpected way. One morning, Alyce received a telephone call from an emergency operator informing her that her next-door neighbor had had an accident and was lying under her Christmas tree unable to free herself. Still in her nightgown, Alyce slipped into a pair of rubber boots, threw on a jacket, and dashed next door to the Landry's house. Without knocking, she threw open the door and ran into their kitchen to rescue her neighbor.

What she saw was not her neighbor helpless under the tree but rather a startled Peggy, her mother, and Peggy's two children whose breakfast was being interrupted by an intruder. Aghast to see such a sight, nobody said a word.

"Oh, my goodness, I'm so sorry. Wrong house. I'm your neighbor, Alyce. No time to explain," Alyce stammered. The Landrys, mouths agape, just nodded.

Alyce quickly slammed the door shut and trudged to Rollene King's house across the mixture of snow-covered dirt piles. "What a way to meet them, in a nightgown and rubber boots. They're probably questioning their move to Katydid now," she lamented.

"Rollene," Alyce shouted as she entered the King's kitchen.

"In here," a raspy voice responded. Entering the living room, Alyce saw the oversized Christmas tree prone on the floor, decorations dangling from its branches and glass ornaments broken.

Suddenly a small head peered around a branch. Alyce saw Rollene, lying under the tree, one hand perilously holding a phone cord.

"Oh Alyce, thank God you're here. I wanted to add a few more ornaments to the top of the tree. I stepped back to see better and tripped. I just grabbed onto the tree branch, but the whole tree came down. I told Pete more than once that we needed a new tree stand."

"Let's just get you up." Alyce grabbed the top branch and slid the tree away from Rollene. Holding Rollene's arms, she hoisted her upright. "Are you okay?" she asked.

"Well, no broken limbs, I guess. Thank goodness the phone has a long cord that I could reach, or I would have been here till the kids came home from school."

A year later in Abington, Luci and Jim Record were outgrowing their small, one-bedroom apartment. Their oldest son, Jimmy, had been sleeping in a very spacious walk-in closet, but it was time for Jimmy to come out of the closet now that Luci was pregnant with their second son Stephen. They had looked at that new Crowley development in Hanson and were very interested. Their realtor had dropped off the binder at the apartment that morning, and the Records planned to revisit the house on the weekend to confirm their selection and sign the binder.

Stephen's unplanned arrival on February 16th changed their plans. While Jim was at work, Stephen signaled his impending arrival, initiating a flurry of activity. Luci called Jim and then her neighbor Susan, who brought young Jimmy to Mrs. Antel's apartment downstairs and then drove Luci to the hospital.

Once notified at work, Jim threw on his topcoat and ran the whole eight minutes to the subway station. Twenty torturous minutes later, he finally departed the subway and found his car. Another half hour elapsed before he nervously arrived at the hospital.

Unfortunately, in those days, husbands were not allowed in the delivery room. Approaching the hospital's information booth, he tried to sound casual as he said, "My wife has been admitted."

"Who's your wife?"

"Luci."

"Sir, what's her last name?"

"Lagarto—I mean Record." Because Jim had been in Vietnam for Jimmy's birth, he was now exhibiting the anxiety usually reserved for first-time fathers.

Finally, Jim was allowed to see Luci and his new son. As the nurse wheeled her out of the delivery room, Jim thought she looked frail and vulnerable, her pocketbook haphazardly tossed beneath the gurney's mattress. Both mother and son showed signs of a long struggle.

Luci smiled through tired eyes, and her voice, though labored, happily exclaimed, "Oh, Jim, a brother for Jimmy."

Relieved and elated, Jim tenderly brushed Luci's hair from her face and beamed. "Worth the wait. With that black eye, he looks like a fighter." Although Stephen's tiny forehead was temporarily marked by forceps, his vocal cords were excellent.

Once in her room and with the baby in the nursery, Luci suddenly stopped, grabbed Jim's arm, and cried, "Oh no. We haven't signed the binder. What if they sell the house to somebody else?"

"That's not important now. Just rest."

"But it is important. Wait. Check my bag. I think I left the binder in my bag."

"Okay." Jim dubiously eyed the rather large pocketbook. "Luci, where do I begin? There are so many zippers."

"They're called compartments to keep things organized. Look in the second zipper from the left. The pens are in the outside compartment."

"Well, it's nice to know all those years of Girl Scouting weren't wasted. You certainly were prepared. I found it."

"Yippee. Let's sign it now, and you can drop it off at Dot Mather's office on your way home. I'm so happy. A healthy baby and a new house! I feel like dancing." Then she winced. "Ah, or maybe we'll have to dance another time."

They signed the binder for 56 Katydid Lane in the Brockton Hospital and moved on May 15, 1971. Daughter Lauren's happy arrival in 1974 completed the Record household.

Moving into a brand-new development has its advantages, especially for mothers with young children. Everyone is new and eager to develop relationships, both for the children and for themselves. Although Alyce had seen Luci speaking to Rollene and Luci's hopes were high when she saw a baby carriage on Alyce's stoop, the first meeting of Alyce and Luci only occurred one sunny June morning a couple of weeks after the Records had moved in. Alyce was pushing baby Allison in her carriage and Luci, holding baby Steve, had just run out to get the mail, a highlight of her day at the time.

Dressed in shorts and an old, paint-stained T-shirt, Luci thought, "Oh, no. What bad luck. The one day I go to pick up the mail in my painting clothes! I look a mess. There she is in a pair of cute shorts and a top. So much for first impressions!"

Approaching Luci's house, Alyce thought, "Ooh, she's young and has a baby that may be Allison's age. What luck!" At the mailbox, Alyce stopped. "Welcome to the neighborhood. I'm Alyce and this is Allison. Sorry I haven't had a chance to stop by earlier."

"Hi Alyce, I'm Luci and this is Stephen. He's just two months old. I've been in a daze the last two weeks moving in. Thank goodness he's a good baby. I'm trying to paint the boys' room first. My older son Jimmy is napping in the living room, so I just ran out to get the mail between paint coats."

"No need to explain. We've been here almost a year, and I still haven't painted all the rooms. I can't believe our babies are just about a year apart. I have three more in the house."

"Yikes, I guess I can't complain about not having any time for myself with only two kids. Do you have time for tea?"

"I'd love it, but I left the three girls playing with my six-year-old in charge. Why don't you stop over after your older boy wakes up from his nap?"

"Sounds great. See you then. Hopefully, I'll have a chance to change out of my paint clothes."

"Don't bother, you just missed me in my paint clothes last week."

Eureka! Over tea, Luci and Alyce quickly discovered that they were both stay-at-home mothers only a year apart in age who loved to cook, were crafty, had the same sense of humor, and had children in the same age range. As the tea brewed, little did they know that many adventures were brewing ahead for these two young mothers.

When the ranch house next to Luci and Alyce finally sold, the gals were eager to meet their new neighbors. Luci called Alyce. "Can you smell the aroma coming from my banana bread? You know what that means. It just came out of the oven and is ready for a welcome wagon visit to the Swensons."

"Wait, I thought you were making the banana bread next week."

"These bananas couldn't wait."

"Okay, but I have to comb my hair and put on lipstick first."

"Lipstick? Are you serious? Oh, is this to be a fancy visit? Well, the banana bread has to cool, so we might as well. The kids are all in the circle anyway."

A tall, smiling man with a bushy mustache greeted them. Joan was at her part-time job at Chadwick's in Brockton and Brad was in charge of the baby for the day. Although Brad invited them in, they knew that leaving the kids playing in the circle without supervision, or worse, taking them all inside, would probably not be wise. After they met Brad, they knew that he and Joan would fit right in on Katydid with their warmth and midwestern affability.

The mix of wonderful neighbors, plenty of playmates for their children, and the natural beauty of their surroundings made Katydid a special place to live and raise children as well as a place to develop lasting friendships and create many memorable adventures.

PART I

The Frazzle Phase: Keeping One Step Ahead of the Katydid Lane Kids

CHAPTER 1

Westward Ho to Ohio With Seven Children Twelve and Under

Alyce and Luci shared good times, good food, and many memories of their early years on Katydid with the Swensons. The three women were the three musketeers of Katydid. The bittersweet news that the Swensons were relocating to Ohio for Brad's new job brought mixed emotions: happiness for Brad but sadness about losing their companions. What were they to do? What chance would they have to see Joan again, with seven children under twelve between the two of them and two husbands with full-time jobs who weren't available to babysit during their visit to Ohio?

This was a time when Girls' Night Out or Girls' Weekends weren't something these young mothers had ever contemplated. But as the separation grew harder, Alyce and Luci fomented a plan. It was outrageous, bold, and daring but doable. They would drive to Ohio with all seven children, the youngest being eighteen-month-old Lauren-Kate, for a visit. Thankfully, Alyce had a 1970 Buick station wagon. It wasn't in the best shape, but these gals were undaunted.

Their husbands tried to use reasonable arguments against the plan: It's too long a ride for two women alone, not to mention with all seven children piled in the car. How were they going to keep the children amused so they wouldn't start to attack each other? Where were they going to stay with all those kids? What would they do if the car broke down?

The ladies had answers for all their concerns.

"We'll only drive during daylight hours," Alyce assured them.

"Very carefully," Luci added. "And we'll bring plenty of games and books for the kids. You know what a good driver Alyce is, and I can give her the directions, so she doesn't have to take her eyes off the road."

Alyce quickly added, "Ron, you know the car is a good, dependable car. We've never had any problems with it."

The gals continued in rapid-fire precision to argue their case. Although Ron and Jim were still concerned, they finally gave in to their enthusiastic and relentless wives after securing promises that the travelers would call them each night. The pilgrimage left Sunday morning for their six-day adventure.

Alyce was the captain of the caravan, and Luci was the navigational officer. This was before smartphones and GPS, so the directional beacon was their map. In those days, maps were large and cumbersome, and once opened, they were impossible to return to their original form.

They decided to go with the route that would take them through Niagara Falls. There is a certain irony about visiting a honeymoon destination with children instead of husbands, but they were undeterred.

Traveling with seven children posed some logistical problems. However, they were able to combat this with frequent stops to eat, and eat they did. The first stop was a picnic off the busy highway. Luckily, the Alyce/Luci team worked well together. In a flash, blankets were placed, the food presented, and the children fed. This well-oiled machine reversed the process just as efficiently, and soon they were back on the road with the children interacting peacefully and Alyce and Luci chatting away.

Picnics on the roadside were followed by breakfasts on hills, knolls, and even dinners in restaurants. One restaurant was the York Steakhouse, a popular and reasonably priced establishment that catered to children and adults. Diners would stand in line, choose what dinner they wanted, and watch it being prepared. Almost all the children ordered hamburgers and fries, a reasonable choice. The last child to order was Karen, aged six and a half, who ordered a half-pound steak, baked potato, and vegetables. Alyce and Luci looked at each other, shrugged their shoulders, and said, "Okay."

The children had fun together and the ladies never ran out of conversation. In fact, Jimmy recalls that they played many car games like "five-letter words" and "new words," and he credits Lauren H for teaching him long division on the trip. Karen and Deedee were excellent babysitters for eighteen-month-old Lauren-Kate, and Steve and Allison were a chatty twosome.

Their first adventure was visiting Niagara Falls. Although the children were tired, the sheer magnitude of the falls captured their interest. What also captured our gals' interest was keeping all seven children within eyesight and on the paved path. Of course, when they were on the bridge and noticed the Maid of the Mist go under the falls, the more adventurous of the group were curious and wanted to hop aboard.

Visions of one or more of the children trying to climb over the boat to get a "better view" made the decision easy to make. Wiser heads prevailed, and the children had to be content to hear the roar of the falls and feel the mist on their faces while standing on terra firma.

Finding a hotel for the night proved more challenging. Luci and Alyce wanted to stay at a hotel with a swimming pool so the children would have a nice way to end their day. At last, as dusk approached, they found a hotel in Dubois, Pennsylvania. Two women with seven children under twelve are not a hotel owner's dream occupants. The clan huddled in the parking lot of the hotel as they formulated a plan. They would take two children in with them, while the rest of the children stayed in the car.

Now, whom should they choose? Lauren, as the oldest, would have to stay in the car to watch the others. What age and gender would appear unthreatening to the hotel? Little Karen with her blond pigtails and quiet demeanor was a natural choice.

"If we explain the problem to Jimmy, he'll know just what to say if asked any questions," opined Luci. Young Jimmy had a reputation for being mature beyond his years. In fact, sometimes he would try to "parent" Steve. It wasn't long before Steve would tell him, "You're not my dad. I already have a dad."

Choices made, they boldly entered the hotel, secured a room, returned to the car, parked in the back, and entered through a back entrance with the rest of the brood. It worked. They were now in what Steve called "our home hotel." On their return to the hotel after dinner, Steve, who was four and a half, saw what he thought was his "home hotel" and insisted he would not go to any other hotel because his pajamas were back in the hotel he had seen. They convinced him that his pajamas were safe and that they would return to the right hotel. Time for bed. Two queen beds and nine sleepers made for strange bedfellows with the oldest in beds and the youngest blanketed on the floor. Eventually, all the children fell asleep.

Content that their motherly duties were complete for the night, Luci and Alyce took advantage of their balcony view of the indoor pool. Ever resourceful, they had brought wine. Plopping down on plastic patio chairs and sipping wine from plastic hotel cups, they relaxed. Alyce turned to Luci with a sigh. "Do you think the children are enjoying this trip as much as we are?"

"Listen, of course they are. Didn't you hear all the chatter as we rode along? They're singing, playing games, and giggling."

"I hope so. I guess there's nothing like a road trip traveling down the highway packed into a car with eight other people and feeling like a sardine to make you feel good."

"You mean *everyone* doesn't squeeze a car seat and three children in the back? Three in the cargo area works. Thank goodness we don't have a sedan. Three children in the trunk would never work. Let's just finish this wine and pretend we are in the Bahamas sipping pina coladas. Refill please."

Their reverie was interrupted by a loud "ow" followed by "oops." A quick check revealed it was just one of the children tripping over another on the way to the bathroom. The rest of the evening passed uneventfully until they awoke early the next morning to huffing and puffing. Steve was completing his morning routine of push-ups and jumping jacks, which he said simply had to be done.

Although only four hours away from their destination, they didn't get an early start. More pool time was a must. Of course, that was followed by a leisurely breakfast and then by packing, which took up the rest of the morning. Taking full advantage of the hotel's late checkout, they started the journey after 11:00 and finally arrived in Worthington, Ohio, late in the afternoon.

The caravan pulled up to the Swenson's house, a beautiful, sprawling California brick ranch. Outside, Brad was waving vigorously to capture their attention. Joan, a broad smile on her face, was as happy to see them as they were to see her. Little Abby, standing next to Joan, was uncertain what the fuss was all about. She saw two women pile out of each side of the car and then a barrage of kids stream from the back of the car.

"Oh, Joan, it's so great to see you again," said Alyce and Luci in unison as they ran to hug her.

"I've been so excited since the day you called and said you both were coming," gushed Joan. "I can't believe how big the kids are. Lauren is taller than you, Alyce."

"Well Joan, having kids reach our height isn't hard," added Luci.

"Let's go inside. I'll show you the house," said Joan.

Both Luci and Alyce oohed and ahhed as they saw the large kitchen that was open to the family room.

"I love how you can see the kids while you're in the kitchen," exclaimed Luci.

"I love the huge windows that bring in so much light," admired Alyce.

The kids were especially excited to see Abby's playroom with a working carousel in the middle of the room. It was a magical room with a closet full of costumes. Soon the children began trying on costumes and riding the carousel. Cowboys and Indians emerged.

Brad, who was interested in biorhythms and transcendental meditation at the time, enthralled the older children as he explained biorhythms and then calculated their biorhythms cycles. The ladies chatted and caught up on each other's interests, recipes, and families.

The next day, the Swensons were eager to take their visitors to the Ohio Caves. The kids learned about stalagmites and stalactites firsthand, especially the Crystal King stalactite, which was estimated to be two hundred thousand years old. After a full day of activities and a hearty supper, the children were ready for bed early, and the adults enjoyed the rest of the evening reminiscing about old times in Katydid, New England, and living in the Midwest. Brad promised a tour of Worthington the next day. Joan was going to stay with the little ones, and Brad would drive the ladies and the older children around.

Wednesday started out a bright day. The older children were glad to be part of the "adult" tour. Suddenly wailing sirens pierced the air. Alyce and Luci looked at each other with trepidation.

Brad quickly reassured them, "It's just a tornado warning. We get those all the time. Nothing to stop our trip."

Twelve-year-old Lauren was old enough to be scared, but Brad was nonchalant, and they threw caution to the wind and off they went.

Worthington was a lovely midwestern town with manicured streets and a busy downtown. Unlike in New England, streets in Worthington were built in an orderly grid. Brad pointed out that the local bank was once a saloon. Although the warning sirens continued, no tornado disturbed the visit, but these cautious New Englanders remained on high alert.

The visit in Ohio passed swiftly, and before long, the time to leave had come. After a tearful goodbye, Alyce and Luci decided to take a different route home. While placing the suitcases in the car, Brad observed, "You know, you have four bald tires."

Alyce quickly assured Brad, "Oh, we will definitely check that out."

Luci echoed, "Absolutely, first chance we get on our way out." Off they went with no intention to slow the journey home. The hotel they found that night was very different from the one in Dubois. No pool, no balcony, no wine, and nine very tired travelers.

They arrived home the next day to the delight of Ron and Jim. Soon the children were back to their routines of playing in the circle and swimming at Cranberry Cove. The car with its bald tires had survived and so had they. The old adage, "Where there's a will, there's a way" became their mantra.

CHAPTER 2

School Daze

When the perfume from a myriad of soap plants wafted through Luci's backyard in early August, the ladies knew it was time to prepare for the first day of school rituals. Shopping for school clothes and school supplies was peppered in between glorious summer days. As Labor Day approached, the New England weather didn't always reflect the upcoming rite of passage. Oftentimes, instead of a brisk fall day, the children faced a balmy seventy-five-degree day dressed in their new school attire.

Gathering in the circle, the tribe of young scholars waited for the big yellow school bus. Oftentimes, they assembled early enough for the girls to get in a quick jump-roping session. When their mothers emerged with Polaroid cameras in hand, the children knew the requisite first-day-of-school picture was inevitable. The mothers quickly corralled errant curls and untucked shirts until a row of freshly scrubbed little faces squirmed before them. Little girls with their hair in upbraids and ribbons wore Polly Flinders dresses and Mary Jane shoes, although Allison always wore pants. Little boys were clad in shirts and plaid bellbottoms and shoes, never sneakers. Nary a pair of torn jeans was observed in those early years.

The little ones were nervous with quivering lips, while the older ones were loving their new outfits and anticipating seeing their friends again. Those children who weren't ready for school were trying to get in the picture with a mixture of awe and fear as the big yellow school bus approached. Over the years those pictures became a metaphor for the fleeting nature of childhood.

In those days, the school bus always came down the street and stopped outside Alyce's house. The children didn't have to wait in the rain nor did parents have to drive or walk them to the top of the street. Now all the students on Katydid must go to the top of the street onto busy Route 58 to get the bus.

As the lumbering yellow behemoth screeched to a stop in the circle, the Katydid mothers waved goodbye, and the children got on the bus with varying degrees of eagerness.

In 1977, waving goodbye was more complicated because Alyce had just given birth to her fifth daughter Jill in July, and Luci still had her three-year-old Lauren-Kate in tow.

Dashing down the street pushing Lauren-Kate in her stroller, Luci exclaimed, "Alyce, I just made it by a hair. Lauren-Kate slept later, which made it easier to get the boys ready, but I didn't have time to shower, so don't get near me."

Alyce, cradling baby Jill, added, "You think that was bad? I was trying to nurse Jill and still fix Karen's hair. What's a shower? And weren't you wearing that outfit yesterday, Luci?"

"What gave it away, the jam spot? It's not easy maintaining a high level of sophistication while you're trying to corral three little ones."

"Gee Luci, I wish they would stay little for a lot longer," Alyce sighed.

"Oh Alyce, I'm getting depressed. I need a cup of tea." They wistfully went in for tea.

As Alyce put baby Jill in her crib, Luci put Lauren-Kate in Alyce's playpen surrounded by baby toys before putting on the teakettle. Coming into the kitchen, Alyce reflected, "I don't know if I'm ready for the next stage when they are independent and out in the world making their own decisions. Lauren wants to wear lipstick and she's only thirteen."

"Gee, she'll be wearing more makeup than we do soon. Let me give Lauren-Kate some Cheerios and we can talk. You realize we only have twenty minutes of Cheerios time," moaned Luci.

"Who knew that when raising our children we would feel fear, delight, and awe," added Alyce as she poured herself another cup of tea.

"Alyce, you seem particularly philosophical today. Do you think it's postpartum?"

"After five kids, I doubt it's postpartum. I can't imagine how hard it must be to suffer with postpartum. I think I'm just realizing how fast the time goes," Alyce sighed.

Luci gave Lauren-Kate more Cheerios and added, "I'm not at that stage yet. I think I'm in the sweet spot where they're all potty-trained, coherent, and play well together. They still like us. I'm not ready to give this moment up."

Alyce lamented, "My Lauren is a teenager with a mind of her own, and Deedee's right on her heels. I know Deedee will test my limits. She started when she was three when she wouldn't accept no from me because she could get a yes from Dad."

"Alyce, you're their role model. You're strong and independent, with a mind of your own but empathetic and caring for others. They are all wonderful girls. They adore you. Keep doing what you're doing. It won't hurt to pray and keep your fingers crossed, though."

"Oh, Luci, you always make me feel better."

"We can only do our best. I'm sure when they are grown, they will tell stories about their childhood that will make us gasp in horror," Luci reluctantly admitted.

From her crib upstairs, Jill announced it was time to eat again, so the back-to-school tea was over.

A very different atmosphere permeated Katydid in June. Now the thundering behemoth screeched to a halt at the circle and raucous laughter and giddiness emerged from the bus with unquestioned eagerness. How the bus driver managed to maintain her hearing in that bus filled with celebratory children eager to voice their pleasure was remarkable.

After report cards were admired and the children changed into play clothes, they all gathered at either Luci or Alyce's house for their culinary treat. The last day of school was always celebrated with a "Make your own Sundae Party." If the weather was good, the party was held outside in Luci's or Alyce's backyard. Picnic tables were strewn with many flavors of ice cream, a variety of sauces, toppings aplenty, and of course mounds of freshly whipped cream and maraschino cherries. It was as much fun watching this chaotic scene for the ladies as it was for the children who created it.

CHAPTER 3

Slippery Slope

"Have you checked the calendar, Alyce? School vacation is only three weeks away," noted Luci as she walked with Alyce around the circle. "Aren't we lucky to get this walk in before the snow arrives tonight," she added, adjusting her scarf.

"I know. It feels like the holiday vacation was just last week. We should do something different this year for the younger kids," said Alyce.

"How about skiing?" suggested Luci.

"You, suggesting skiing? I'm impressed."

"Well, I'm trying to think beyond my comfort zone. I didn't think a trip to the library for new books would spark their interest. Plus, it's something both the boys and the girls would like."

"Ooh, that's good. We could take a lesson too," Alyce eagerly added.

"Yes, Alyce. We could be role models for trying new things. We could start organizing it now."

"Let's finish walking, and then we'll go in and plan," said Alyce.

It didn't take long to organize their trip with the younger children to Pat's Peak in New Hampshire.

The day was lovely, not too cold, and the sky was clear. They stopped to eat breakfast at a small restaurant in New Hampshire, but it was taking an inordinate amount of time for the pancake breakfast to arrive for a very anxious group of eager young skiers.

Our gals were quite content to linger over a hot cup of coffee, but even they became curious as to the delay because the restaurant wasn't overly crowded and they weren't offering free food. Then they noticed that the waitresses were short of breath, and there was always a cool blast of air when they came from the "kitchen." They soon realized that the kitchen was in another building, and the wait staff had to run between buildings to bring the food. At last, the food was served, eaten, and paid for, and the well-fed travelers continued their trek.

After arriving at the mountain, they geared up and the children headed for the chair lifts. "Stay safe and have fun," both mothers chimed.

"Okay, Alyce, it's our turn to ski."

"We have to get these skis on first," said Alyce as she sat on the bench.

Luci tried to maintain her balance as she held the wall with one hand and tried to snap her boot into the ski with her foot. "This isn't as easy as I thought. I think my skis are too long,"

Alyce sighed. "I'm exhausted just getting into gear and we haven't started skiing."

"See, Alyce, we're already getting exercise."

Alyce just rolled her eyes. Twenty minutes later they were ready for their ski lesson.

Forty-five minutes later, they were told, "You're ready for the lift. Have fun." According to their teenage instructor, they had all the necessary skills to go up the lift and down the bunny slope by themselves. Having seen their novice performances, it's remarkable that their instructor kept a straight face.

Alyce was the first to head down this slippery slope. However, with her poles flailing in the air, she began speeding out of control.

What had her teenage instructor told her to do? "She said to snowplow," Alyce remembered. "Oh God, I can't make these sticks attached to the bottom of my boots snowplow," she groaned.

The tips of her skis were now crisscrossed over each other and in no way was she slowing down. Instead, she faced two choices: either snowplow into a two-hundred-year-old pine tree or a two-year-old skier.

Miraculously, both the tree and the two-year-old survived her. With her poles aimed over her head, she continued down the slope. Once Alyce was at the bottom of the bunny hill, the instructor approached and decided to take Alyce's poles away, adding, "Don't get discouraged, a lot of people your age have difficulty at first."

"But I'm only forty," she thought, "Who knew I'd go downhill that fast?"

Unfortunately, Luci's first skiing experience was no better. Because she's afraid of heights, going up the lift proved the first challenge. It got worse. She fell off the J bar. With encouragement from her teenage instructor, she tried again. As the ground receded below, she realized that what goes up, must come down. How was she getting off this contraption?

"What if I can't slide off? Skis slide down," she worried. Why she hadn't realized that skis were meant to slide down defies logic.

Suddenly, she couldn't remember how to stop the skis—something like crossing skis, she thought. As she catapulted out of the seat into the arms of a helpful ski employee, she was quickly escorted away from the lift so the next skier could easily transition from J bar to slope. Luci was sure that the skier was a very small adult because that couldn't have been a child who accomplished the feat so gracefully.

Buoyed that she was off the J bar, she posited, "It can't be that hard to get down. It's not the Alps, for heaven's sake. It's the bunny slope."

Alas, that quick burst of confidence didn't last long, and the trip down was an adrenaline-filled trip. Unlike most skiers who avoid trees, Luci was hoping that she could find a tree to hold on to. She contemplated taking her skis off and walking down the slope, but her pride would not accept that choice. Needless to say, she fell numerous times.

Nearing the end of the slope, the incline was slight. She tried to regain her composure because she didn't want to come down screaming like a banshee. Standing upright, her chin high, she took a deep breath. She was going to do it.

For the first few seconds it looked good until, out of nowhere, a little four-year-old was in her path. In her head she was screaming, "Get out of the way, I can't stop." But nothing came out, and she plowed into the child, who fell, crying.

"Oh, sorry, so sorry," she cried and quickly exited. She found Alyce.

"How was it, Luci?"

"Frightening. My mind wanted to ski, but my body made a strong case against it. I rather like having all my bones in their customary spot. The body won."

"Me too. Maybe we should have started with cross-country skiing instead of downhill," Alyce offered.

"Well, at least we tried. I could go for a nice hot chocolate now," suggested Luci.

"Agreed. Let's find a seat near the fireplace. It's kinda cold outside when you're not skiing."

The lodge was much more accommodating with its crackling fire and concession stand. Armed with hot chocolate, they found window seats close enough to the fireplace to feel its warmth and still observe the skiers. They sat and watched the skiers for over an hour before Alyce saw some familiar faces. "Look Luci, there's Lauren-Kate and Jill skiing on the bunny slope."

"Wow, they are actually skiing," exclaimed Luci.

"Oh, Luci, look at our rosy-cheeked kids laughing and having so much fun." Alyce beamed. "If we could have been more proficient, we could have been out there with them."

"More proficient? We never made it down one hill successfully. We need more lessons."

Suddenly, Lauren-Kate and Jill burst through the lodge door and approached the mothers breathlessly, tripping over each other and giggling. Luci asked, "Are you all done, girls?"

"No way," gushed Lauren-Kate.

"We're so cold. We need to warm up and have hot chocolate," added Jill.

"How do you girls like skiing?" said Alyce as she reached into her pocket for money.

"I've got it," said Luci who had already reached into her pocket.

"No, no, I don't want you paying for this," argued Alyce as she pushed in front of Luci.

Not to be outdone, Luci lunged forward and hurled money at

Lauren-Kate. "You drove, Alyce, so I'm not letting you pay," demanded Luci.

The girls, concerned a melee would ensue, reached out for the money and ran to the concession stand, yelling, "Thanks."

Meanwhile, Steve and Jimmy were skiing the green and blue slopes. Jimmy remembers he was wearing suede fur-lined gloves which he said, "feels good against my face when I'm too cold." By 4:00 p.m., four tired but happy skiers joined their mothers at the lodge.

The trip back home was fun filled with the children remarking how "easy" and "fun" skiing was. From the front seat, Alyce and Luci just looked at each other and continued to sip their cups of hot chocolate.

CHAPTER 4

The Kids, the Camp, and the Cove

When the first house was built on Katydid Lane, two unique pieces of property were near the new development: Camp Kiwanee and Cranberry Cove. In 1979, the Campfire Girls' Camp offered to sell Camp Kiwanee to the town. Katydid Lane residents rallied at town hall meetings to ensure that the town bought the sixty-eight-acre property. For $185,000, the town acquired a spring-fed pond, a fully functioning camp, and many beautiful natural areas to hike. It was a no-brainer.

Originally, the lodge at the camp had been the summer estate of Albert Burrage, a prominent Boston lawyer. "The Needles," as the lodge was called, was built between 1899 and 1906. Burrage sold the property to the Boston Chapter of Camp Fire Girls in 1929 on a whim because he thought that the Town of Hanson was charging him too much money in taxes. Rumors that the lodge was haunted only added to its mystique. For a few years, the lodge became a haunted house to entertain the town folk on Halloween.

Abutting Camp Kiwanee was Cranberry Cove, which had been gifted to the town by Marcus Urann, a cranberry magnate. Cranberry Cove had been operating as a town beach since the 1940s. Both Cranberry Cove and Camp Kiwanee shared a single-lane paved road lined with trees. Now, with the purchase of Camp Kiwanee, the entire sixty-eight acres would become a recreational area for town residents.

The Cove was a treasure trove for these young swimmers. Trees surrounded the pond, lending an air of serenity and security. The two docks, one H and one I, spelled out HI, providing a welcoming message to the swimmers. Springboards for diving at the end of both the H and the I docks added to the swimming experience. A test of swim team members' endurance and a hallmark of their skills was the one-mile swim to the island in the middle of the pond. Many past members of the swim team became lifeguards who enthusiastically carried on the rich tradition of excellence at the Cove. The Cove consistently produced medal-winning swim teams for Hanson.

The Cove came with strict rules. Oftentimes the sound of a whistle blowing and a loud, "No running on the docks" or "no pushing" would be heard. Afternoons gave way to open swim. Roped-off boundaries delineated the areas for the diverse swim levels. Babies sat on the sandy lake edge splashing the water while more accomplished swimmers were jumping off the docks, tossing a ball, or playing with their friends.

Then the dreaded whistle blew. Begrudgingly, all the children came out of the water. The fifteen-minute adult swim commenced. For Alyce, that meant she could enjoy a peaceful swim in the crystal-clear water. For Luci, it meant sitting on the dock with water lapping at her feet.

The town offered residents swimming lessons from beginner to lifeguard certification at Cranberry Cove. Additionally, synchronized swimming, snorkeling, and diving lessons were available. In the 70s and 80s, all these activities were free. For Katydid mothers, their proximity to the Cove became a natural opportunity to sign up their children for as many of these activities as possible.

Alyce and Luci would take their young charges, hand-in-hand, to the beach. The path, designed for one-way traffic with no pedestrian walkway, required these mothers and their little ones to make quick moves to huddle among the trees whenever a car passed.

Those short walks became adventures for the children. Along the route, a few feet into the trees lay an old family burial plot. Eager to explore the weather-beaten tombstones, tiny hands tugged their mothers forward toward the short brush. Unable to read the names, the children tried to imagine who these people were.

Farther down the path, a fallen, moss-covered tree limb, resembling an alligator, canopied over a little stream. A carved-out hill among the trees offered the children another challenge as they raced ahead before their lessons began.

Once they arrived at the Cove, the children ran to their lessons. The young mothers spread out blankets and sat for hours on the soft sand. Luci turned to Alyce and whispered, "I can't believe we get to relax in the sun for hours and they call it minding the children. How lucky we are. They're thoroughly occupied and learning a life skill."

"Are you serious?" Alyce retorted. "We earned this after birthing these children and changing all those diapers. I think a day in the sun is well deserved."

"Ooh, Alyce. You rebel. Didn't you change all those diapers with love in your heart?" Luci cajoled.

Their banter was soon interrupted when neighbors Maggie and Brenda joined them. "Hi girls," said Maggie. "You both got here early today. Great blanket location to observe the scenery." She winked. Her comment, a veiled reference to one young male lifeguard, who always wore his skimpy swim team Speedo, drew muffled laughter from these usually demure mothers. Those idyllic summer days, however, came to a halt when the children were old enough to walk to the Cove themselves.

All the children became great swimmers. This was especially important to Luci because she hadn't learned to swim as a child. Plagued by a fear of water, she was determined not to pass on that fear. She only took swimming lessons in her thirties, but that's another story.

Both the Hennelly and Record children were on the Hanson Swim Team, members of the competitive league of South Shore towns. That meant practices every day and races against neighboring towns.

Technically, Jimmy wasn't officially a member. He didn't have to go to practices. Only when they were short a swimmer for a race did they ask Steve to "call your brother." Jimmy claims he wasn't a great swimmer and says his greatest accomplishment was a third-place finish in one race. But he always answered the call.

All the Hennelly girls and Steve racked up medals on the swim team. Steve's favorite event was the backstroke where his powerful shoulders brought him several wins. Lauren Hennelly was the queen of the backstroke, and Deedee was the master of the breaststroke. The swim and diving teams were a force to be reckoned with in competition. After a season of weekend races, some of the members, including Lauren, Deedee, Karen, and Allison would go to the pool at Bridgewater State University campus and compete against other Massachusetts teams to qualify for the State Championship. Allison and Karen competed in the individual medley. This event featured breast, back, butterfly, and freestyle.

The end of the season for the swim classes meant a cookout followed by the presentation of certificates of advancement, including lifeguard certification for the older swimmers. They had passed all requirements, including avoiding the Cove's resident snapping turtle, Bruce. For Luci's Lauren-Kate, her fear of Bruce was so great it was remarkable that she ever learned to swim at all.

The synchronized swim team culminated the end of their season with a late afternoon water ballet performance. Strains of classical music from *Romeo and Juliet* or the soothing sounds of Kenny Rogers singing "Lady" greeted the audience of parents and friends as they entered. Placing blankets on the sand, the parents were eager to watch their budding Esther Williamses.

When the music slowed, they announced the show was about to begin. As the sun set and the water glistened, the children dove in and out of the water in unison to the rhythm of the music, creating an evening in harmony with the spheres. Many proud parents, removed from the complexities of adult life for a brief interlude, swayed in solidarity to the gracefulness and beauty of the performance.

CHAPTER 5

Rocking the Block

Dressed in workout clothes, Alyce and Luci began running around the circle, their latest exercise and a metaphor for their busy lives at the time. One morning Bob Madison, his new camcorder anchored on his shoulder, approached and began filming. Because neither woman wanted her running to be captured for posterity, they tried to distract him with conversation. When Bob mentioned a recent block party he had attended with friends, both women looked at each other. "Great idea. Let's have one here," and the yearly Katydid Block Party was born.

The cul-de-sac was the perfect venue for such an event. The families that surrounded the cul-de-sac provided the grills. Katydid men would set up picnic tables early in the morning. José Monteiro would haul down a refrigerator and long extension cords. Ron Hennelly would set up a stereo system for music, bring trash barrels, and set up the lights. Luci and Alyce gathered the props for the games, and Bob Madison brought his camcorder and whistle.

Each family brought their own hamburgers or hot dogs and a dish to share, creating a bountiful feast for all. There were assorted salads, fruit bowls galore, watermelon, Jell-O molds, and many desserts from brownies to pies. Of course, Peggy Landry would always make her famous homemade Boston baked brown beans.

Both adults and children played games. Three-legged races, sack races, and baseball were among the choices. Seeing the adults in the three-legged race was hilarious, as the height difference between couples made it more of a test of marital equanimity, particularly with the Hennelly and Record couples. Both Alyce and Luci were a foot shorter than their respective husbands, making balance and forward movement challenging. Jimmy and Steve dominated the three-legged race.

In 1976, to honor the Olympic broad jump event, the boys created the "broad smile event." Using a sewing machine tape, Jimmy measured smiles as each child grinned his or her widest. Jimmy says that Greg King won because he had the biggest face.

The egg race with spoons and the egg toss games were also popular. The agile children made contests competitive, but the adults left most of their eggs splattered in the circle, necessitating frequent hosing of the asphalt.

One of the favorite competitions was the pie-eating contest. This was a contest for the children who were oblivious to the ramifications of eating blueberry pie. The adults realized stained teeth, stained clothes, and blue faces, not to mention the laundry dilemma, were some of the consequences of participating in blueberry pie contests.

Individual blueberry pies lined one of the picnic tables. When Bob Madison blew his whistle, our eager contestants dove into the pies, their noses covered in blueberries. Most were unrecognizable at the end of the contest, just two eyes surrounded by blueberry-covered faces.

Another memorable event was the very competitive obstacle course race between Ron Hennelly and Buddy Gill. A chalk line in front of Alyce's driveway was the starting point. The challenge was to run through obstacles strewn along the route around the circle and arrive back at the chalk line.

The contestants had to overcome three obstacles. Firstly, they had to run through the center of six tires staggered in three rows of two, one leg in each tire. Secondly, they had to hold on to the handle of an exercise ball without falling off. Thirdly, they had to crawl through a cardboard box tunnel. Poised at the starting line, these middle-aged athletes were confident. Six-foot-one Ron and five-foot-seven Buddy each claimed they'd be triumphant.

"You'll never be able to stretch your legs to fit in the tires, Buddy," laughed Ron.

"Oh yeah, well let's see how you make out balancing the ball with your long legs," chortled Buddy.

"On your mark, get set, go," shouted Bob Madison.

Ron's right leg slipped into the first tire, while his left leg easily stretched to the matching tire on the left. He quickly repeated the motion to the next set of tires, and then the third set. Not to be outdone, Buddy moved the right tire over to the left side making it easier to place both legs into their respective tires, and then he repeated the steps. It looked like an easy win for Ron.

Momentum began to shift during the exercise ball challenge. Ron's long legs became a handicap, and he struggled to stay on the ball. Buddy, his legs manageably accessing the ground, bounced along nicely, even after Ron tried to grab his shirt to hold him back.

The makeshift cardboard tunnel was next. On hands and knees, they shimmied through with each man guilty of pulling his opponent's legs. This misdemeanor was barely noticed over the laughter from the audience and contestants alike. In the end, a tie was called so both good sports could claim bragging rights.

Music played throughout the day. As soon as a song played on the stereo, Ron would announce, "Ladies' choice," but the ladies were always too busy organizing the food or games to take him up on his offer, though the music did get some of the little ones to dance. His camera ever perched on his shoulder; Bob Madison continued to immortalize these events.

The party continued into the evening. As the young children reached their bedtimes, the ladies took them home while the men stayed, drank beer, and talked sports in the circle.

How different that was from today's new modern mindset. Now the men may be the ones to take the children in and leave the ladies to sip wine and chat about sports.

CHAPTER 6

Bonnie and Clyde Come to Katydid

A reign of terror came to their little neighborhood one summer in 1982 in the most unlikely form of two little partners in crime. Five-year-old Jill Hennelly and Teddy Madison were friends from the beginning. Teddy would walk across the circle to visit her while she sat in her front yard in her baby walker. They were soulmates immediately. When you saw one, you always saw the other.

That summer, Jill and Teddy noticed a family of cement ducks displayed on the lawn of Patrick and Peggy Landry's yard. "Hmmm, what great fun it would be to bury them," they thought, and so they did. Patrick searched the yard, but those ducks were never seen again.

These scalawags, however, were not done causing grief to the Landrys. To quench their thirst, they took a sip of water from the Landry's garden hose and neglected to shut the water off. Unfortunately, Patrick and Peggy were on vacation and returned a week later to a flooded cellar.

The two little ones, now known as Bonny and Clyde, went to visit one of their friends up the street, Joey, who had just received a new little red wagon for his birthday. Their inquisitive minds immediately went to work disassembling his new toy. When they tried to reassemble the wagon, pieces were missing and now lost in the grass.

Joey's father was irate and banned them from the yard for the rest of the summer. That lasted about two weeks when he relented and allowed them back to swim in his new in-ground swimming pool. One afternoon, Joey's mother and father joined the children to watch them swim. Joey's father put on some music. As Jill swam by, her little head popped out of the water and she asked, "Is that Simon and Garfunkel?"

"Yes," said the father, impressed with Jill's musical taste. A common bond over music was made and all was forgiven.

On another occasion, they went exploring the wetlands between their two houses. Poles in hand, they plodded through the grass expecting to find baby bunnies or frogs. Suddenly, one of the poles pierced a hornet's nest and a few hornets swarmed around them, quickly followed by a few more. Flailing their little arms frantically, these young adventurers tried to shoo them away, but there were too many.

Running was their next option. Straight to Teddy's front door they ran, yelling and screaming, a swarm of hornets trailing them. Teddy's mom, seeing their predicament, began to shoo the hornets away, again to no avail. Teddy ran upstairs while his mother and Jill ran downstairs for reinforcements. Teddy's sisters grabbed bed pillows and began wailing on Jill to rid her of the hornets. Utter chaos ensued as the family battled the remaining hornets in the house. Fourteen bites later, the two little explorers limped off to bed that night.

These young firecrackers weren't done with their escapades. One hot summer evening, Jill and Teddy and a package of matches, a lethal combination, headed into the bogs. Soon after their arrival, flames were seen shooting up into the air behind the Record house. The Records had finished dinner and were watching TV when Luci asked, "Jim, did we leave the grill on? I smell smoke."

Jim looked up, noticed the fire, and ran barefoot to get the hose. "Call the fire department. The trees are on fire."

The Record children ran to the window, both excitement and fear in their eyes. "The fire department will take care of it. It'll be okay," Luci nervously assured the children as she dialed 911. Suddenly, she looked up to see a curly-haired little boy and a very small girl with blond braids matching him step by step. "No way," thought Luci. "How am I going to tell Alyce her five-year-old is going to need counseling?"

Within minutes after the fire department arrived, the fire was extinguished with little damage to the conifers. The firemen questioned Jim and Luci, but Luci didn't reveal her suspicions and the culprits remained unidentified. Soon after, however, Jill and Teddy were identified as the perpetrators. Alyce and Ron brought Jill back to the firemen to apologize for what she had done. Teddy's parents restricted him to the circle for an entire week. This cramped their style a bit, but the neighbors got a little reprieve from these curious little imps.

Talking to Luci the next day, Alyce regretfully acknowledged Jill's part in the fire. "Oh, my Lord, imagine if the fire had gotten out of control and burned down the upper knoll area. I don't know if I ever would have been able to face Jim again. The thought of him looking at his scorched earth for years to come instead of his beautiful conifers would have been devastating."

"Alyce, no worries," Luci assured her. "In fact, I've never seen Jim run so fast to save his plants. The man was on a mission. Thankfully, it was easily contained. I told him it was good for the soil, like a contained burn. He didn't buy that, but he's already been to Wyman's to replace one of the plants, so all's good."

Wrestling with Embarrassment

One summer day, Johnny King and Allison Hennelly were watching the two eight-year-olds, Sean Anderson and Steve Record, wrestle. Neither boy actually knew how to wrestle, nor had they ever taken wrestling in school. This was a free-for-all type of wrestling with no real winner, no headgear, and no uniforms, just two young boys tossing and tumbling and trying to pin each other.

Dressed in shorts and T-shirts, their bare legs flailing, these eager wrestlers continued for several minutes on the damp grass. Divots of grass occasionally flew up as knees became scraped and grass-stained. Like tumbleweeds on the plain, their positions changed frequently.

While Johnny encouraged this exhibit of manly athleticism, Allison soon tired of the antics and walked home.

Soon after Allison left, the boys stopped wrestling and ruled the match a tie. Johnny started laughing.

"What's funny?" asked Steve.

Johnny was laughing hard as he blurted out, "Dude, while your legs were up, Allison saw everything. I mean everything."

Steve turned bright red, "No way," he countered. The subject was changed quickly, and they turned their attention to other things. But Steve never forgot. He couldn't be sure. He continued to believe that he had been exposed to a girl. Horrors!

It wasn't until he was an adult that he could laugh and share this embarrassing moment with his mom. Although Luci knew that Steve had turned embarrassed thoughts into humorous ones, the mere thought that her son had suffered even a moment of embarrassment made Luci determined to investigate. The next time she saw Allison, she causally mentioned the incident to her. Allison had no recollection of the incident. Obviously, it had not scarred her for life and confirmed that Steve's privacy and dignity remained intact.

CHAPTER 7

Christmas Innocence Lost

Beyond the religious significance of Christmas, a lot of the magic of Christmas for little children comes from the belief in Santa Claus. At seven years old, Luci's Lauren-Kate still believed.

Perhaps the truth is that parents want to hold onto that innocent belief in Santa Claus as much as the children do. That jolly, red-suited personage represents the idea that giving to others brings joy and that goodness is recognized. Many a mother would use the concept as a moral crutch in the hectic days preceding Christmas, her to-do list growing longer and longer and her patience growing shorter and shorter. "Santa's watching," became a frequent refrain. Nowadays, young mothers have the Christmas Elf on the Shelf to notice when children are "naughty or nice."

Storage of Christmas gifts was one drawback for these parents. Because Lauren-Kate's dad Jim remembered his childhood days of searching for presents, finding them, and then rewrapping them, he was very helpful in assisting Luci in hiding presents. They had bought Lauren-Kate her first "big girl" bike, a beautiful blue number with a little white basket in front. Now she would be able to join the "big kids" riding around the circle and even going up the street with a two-wheeler instead of trailing behind on her tricycle.

They picked up the bike a few days before Christmas. One evening after the children were asleep, Jim brought the bike over to the Gills for safekeeping. This wasn't a problem because the children were in school for the rest of the week and Christmas was over the weekend.

These beleaguered parents hadn't counted on a snowstorm to cancel school that Friday or that Maura and Lauren-Kate would be playing in the Gills' basement. Lauren-Kate noticed the bike but thought it was either Maura's or her sister's. As the girls talked about getting out of school early for Christmas vacation, Lauren-Kate asked Maura what she had asked Santa for. Maura laughed. "You know there's no Santa Claus, right? Our parents buy the gifts."

Confused, but trying to sound grown up to her more worldly year-older friend, she blurted. "Sure, I was kidding."

Yet when Lauren-Kate returned home, she did not confront her parents with their ongoing prevarication. Instead, more questions percolated. "What else haven't they told me? There's probably no Easter Bunny either," she mumbled under her breath.

In her heart of hearts, she hoped Maura was wrong. But that Christmas when she found a beautiful blue bike with a white basket, she knew the truth. Elated that the bike was hers, she thanked her parents.

"But that's from Santa," Luci replied.

"I know there's no Santa. What do you think I am, a baby?"

Luci and Jim were so disappointed. This necessitated the "Spirit of Santa talk." The boys were relieved they no longer had to pretend for Lauren-Kate's sake.

CHAPTER 8

Bumps, Bruises, and Emergency Trips

Blue Bike Blues

With the number of children on Katydid, it was impossible to avoid accidents. There were cuts and bruises, scarred knees, bee stings, and bloody noses. All the mothers kept their medicine cabinets fully stocked, often taking advantage of having Maggie Gill, a registered nurse, as a neighbor.

Because Katydid Lane was a cul-de-sac, riding bikes was a popular activity. The circle at the end of the street was wide and unencumbered. In the 70s and 80s, no one came down the street except the residents. Of course, the definition of "riding my bike" is interpreted differently by parents and children. Racing their bikes was more like it. The slight downward angle from the top of the street made for perfect acceleration culminating in a screeching spin in the broad cul-de-sac. As soon as spring banished winter snow, the bikes emerged.

Seven-year-old Lauren-Kate was anxious to prove she could be as fast as the bigger kids. These were the days before helmets. Lauren-Kate, confident after going up and down Katydid successfully, decided she was ready for the King's driveway. Unlike most of the level driveways on the street, the King's driveway was quite steep.

Lauren-Kate was unprepared for the precipitous decline and crashed the bike at the bottom of the driveway. From inside her house, Luci heard a screech followed by an ear-piercing scream and quickly looked out the window.

She saw brothers Jimmy and Steve running from their driveway up to the King's driveway. Juan Monteiro was running toward the Record house cradling Lauren-Kate in his arms, her face covered in blood. The pained look on Juan's face showed his concern.

Luci was out the door, trying to hold back her tears. "Oh, Juan, thank you," said Luci as she quickly tried to reassure a crying Lauren-Kate. "It's going to be okay. Let's get it checked out." Her voice projected an assurance she didn't feel.

Turning to thirteen-year-old Jimmy, Luci said, "I'm going to take Lau to be checked. Take Steve and go home until I get back. Call Dad and tell him Lau fell off her bike and I'm taking her to the doctor. Tell him she's fine and I'll call him when I get back. If you need anything, call Mrs. Hennelly and don't leave the house while I'm gone."

Gently putting Lauren-Kate in the car, she sped to South Shore Hospital. After several hours in the emergency room, Luci brought her very tired, swollen-faced daughter home. Jimmy and Steve met her at the car.

"Dad has called two times to see if you were back," said Jimmy. As Lauren-Kate got out of the car, she noticed her wide-eyed brothers staring at her solicitously and without their usual sibling banter.

As they entered the house, Lauren-Kate shouted, "Why are you looking at me like that?" She took a quick look in the hall mirror and dashed up the stairs, her crying escalating with each stair. A slammed door announced she was in her room.

Mustering her most self-assured voice, Luci yelled up the stairs, "I know it's hard to eat. How about a popsicle?" Not waiting for a response, she reached into the freezer, grabbed a grape popsicle, and took the stairs two at a time to Lauren-Kate's room. After softly knocking, Luci gingerly entered and sat on the bed. "It looks much worse than it is. The swelling will be down in a couple of days and your teeth are fine. You were very brave to try that steep driveway, especially with your new bike."

As Lauren-Kate's head popped up from under the pillow, she

whimpered, "I ruined my new bike. Now they'll all laugh at me and call me a baby." Back under the pillow she went. Suddenly, she sat up, punched the pillow, and moaned, "It hurts when I lie on my face."

Luci offered the grape popsicle. "Try this, it's your favorite." Putting her arm around her daughter, she added, "You know Lau, the bike can be fixed or replaced. It's not important. You are what's important. You can't let anyone tell you who you are or stop you from trying to do something difficult. This time the driveway beat you, but the next time, you'll beat the driveway. Nobody goes through life without getting bruises, but the key is to pick yourself up and keep trying. You're strong." Giving her a hug, Luci added, "Besides, you look fierce now."

Seconds after Luci spoke with Jim, she called Alyce. "Oh, Alyce. I was so scared. There was so much blood. First thing I did was check her teeth."

"She's going to be fine," comforted Alyce.

"Of course, but my first instinct was never to let her ride a bike again and keep her in bubble wrap."

"Boy, it's tempting to wrap them in bubble wrap or keep them on a leash. What a delicate tightrope we walk when raising children. We can't protect them from everything."

"Oh, Alyce." Luci sighed. "Will we make it through their childhoods without a nervous breakdown?"

"One day at a time. Look, our parents survived raising us," assured Alyce.

Johnny and the Wrist Rocket

In 1985, Sean Anderson and Steve Record built an elaborate fort between the Record and Anderson backyards. At fourteen years old, the boys wanted this fort to be an early version of what today would be called a "man cave." The fort had three stories. Boards of various sizes made up the first two floors. A confiscated old hose found in the Record garage was artfully placed on the top branch of the fort. Thus, the third "floor" was created. The hose became a bungee to slide down, somewhat like a fireman's pole.

Standing on the top branch, the young explorers looked out at the bog that offered changing seasonal vistas. In cranberry harvesting season, the bogs were ablaze with bright red berries. To harvest the crop, water flooded the bogs. The berries floated to the top creating a softly undulating carpet of red. The reds, oranges, and yellows of the surrounding foliage provided a beautiful backdrop. From that perch, the boys could also see the lake behind the bog, the sun glistening like little stars in the water galaxy. Later that year, Hurricane Gloria wiped out most of their fort but before then, there were many adventures.

One particular adventure involved Johnny King and his new wrist rocket, a revolutionary type of slingshot. It incorporated a wrist brace to transfer the force from the wrist to the forearm while shooting. When the bands were pulled with a brace, more force, or torque, was produced, and a steadier, more accurate shot could be made with almost surgical precision. The wrist rocket could shoot a hundred feet.

Steve examined the rocket with admiration. "Cool. It's a beauty. How does it work?"

Johnny boasted, "Watch this. I'm going to hit that big tree." Aiming at a large pine about fifty feet into the bog, Johnny launched his ten-inch arrow into the tree, but the arrow snapped in half. He quickly grabbed the remaining half arrow and pulled it back, but it did not extend past his hand. Now it was near his wrist or forearm. Suddenly gravity took hold, and the arrow plunged into the space between his thumb and his forefinger.

"Yeeouwee," screamed Johnny, holding his arrow-lodged hand. Steve and he exchanged wide-eyed glances. "I gotta get home." Both boys were off the fort in record time and across the street to Johnny's house. They ran, climbing the stoop two steps at a time with Johnny heralding his announcement, "Mom, I've had an accident," before they even got to the kitchen.

Rollene immediately went into mother mode. "Get into the car." The car was out of the driveway before Steve, alone in the kitchen, could even close the door and walk home. As he slowly approached his house, Steve tried to think of how he was going to explain this latest event to his mom.

The vacuum was running when Steve arrived home. He wanted to avoid talking about what happened and tried to go to his room unnoticed. Unfortunately, eagle-eyed mothers have danger radar. Luci turned off the vacuum when she saw him. "Are you okay? You're as white as a ghost."

"I'm fine," he said in his lowest, most masculine voice. "Johnny had a little accident with his new wrist rocket, so he went home."

"His what? Anything that has rocket added to it can't be okay."

Trapped, Steve had no way out and explained what happened, trying to focus on how safe ten-inch arrows are in the hands of four-teen-year-old boys. It didn't work.

"That's a weapon," his mother shouted. "You boys could have been seriously hurt."

"Mom, we're practically adults. We were careful."

"Practically," Luci retorted, "is the operative word, and it doesn't sound like careful is the best word for what happened. I don't have a problem with archery, but I do have a problem with unsupervised arrow-shooting on a perilous perch above ground and aiming at odd targets."

"Oh, Mom, you worry too much."

"That's my job. It's in my DNA."

A couple of days later when Luci and Alyce were having tea, Luci shared the wrist rocket story with her. "Alyce, why do boys always test the limits of danger? Growing up with two sisters, we never did anything dangerous. We played with dolls and paper dolls or played school."

"Yeah," Alyce chuckled, "You found your danger in books."

"Well, at least the danger was only a paper cut. My mother always kept us on a short leash. I don't want to do that with my children. So, I guess I'll just have to get used to it. How about another cup of tea?"

CHAPTER 9

The Wide, Wide World of Sports

Sports activity on Katydid was marked by two distinct periods. In the early 70s, girls dominated the playing population with six girls versus three boys. Given the girls' height advantage, ages, and sheer number, the three boys never questioned a girl's ability to compete.

When the next group of young athletes began playing in the late 70s, the numbers had shifted. Although the numbers remained six to three, this time the boys dominated the playing field. However, these young boys resisted the new arrivals. They hadn't left that stage of development where they thought girls had "cooties" and weren't fit competition.

These girls possessed not only beauty and brains but also athletic ability. After seeing the girls play, the boys quickly learned that girls were indeed quite competitive. The battle of the sexes was over, and the glass ceiling was broken.

Not all the girls found competitiveness a top priority though, as seven-year-old Allison found out when she and eight-year-old Karen first started playing kickball against the boys. From an early age, one of Karen's endearing qualities was her unfailing response whenever Ron came home from work. She would stop whatever she was doing and run to kiss him hello. The ladies and Ron loved that. Allison didn't find it as endearing the day they were playing kickball on the same team. The score was tied, and Karen, now up, could bring in the winning run. Tension was mounting as Karen came to kick.

Suddenly, Ron's car came down the street. "Daddy!" Karen beamed as she put the ball down and began chasing the car into the driveway. Allison, aghast at her sister's lack of priorities, was all in a tizzy as she saw her opportunity to win the game turn into a forfeit.

Competitiveness, however, was always a priority in the lower forty games. The "lower forty" was the affectionate appellation given to the lower part of the Record yard, an alternative site to Manny's backyard for baseball games. First base was the swing set slide, which had long since lost its relevancy for these growing boys. Second base was the big swamp birch tree, and third base was whatever they drew with their shoes. Third base was often debated, especially on tag plays. Home plate was the bottom of the steps leading to the lower forty.

The biggest problem was the lack of fill in that area, which left the roots of dead trees exposed. Jimmy later said he made the all-star team purely out of fear because Manny Monteiro was much stronger. When Manny hit a grounder, you never knew where it was going to pop up. Two choices were available to the young fielder: develop reflexes or risk losing teeth. Another problem was the tree branches that impeded any fly balls. Sometimes baseballs would pinball off the trees.

A third problem was "the moat," a section in the Record's yard that was always swampy in the spring, the perfect area for Manny to hit the ball and a terrible place to try to catch it. Many a baseball game ended with wet socks and squeaky sneakers for Jimmy.

When they weren't playing baseball, the boys were playing basketball, a favorite sport of the Record family. Eager to join the game, Manny and Juan installed a piece of plywood with a metal rim hoop to the telephone pole near his house. The metal had a net that never lasted. Many disputes with Manny occurred because he claimed that all his shots went through even if they were wide of the mark.

After a few years, the weathered backboard developed a pronounced bounce, which made it challenging when they played in school with a hoop that *didn't* bounce. In most games, it was Manny and Jim against Steve and Juan, and a lot of fouling took place. It wasn't an equitable playing field because Manny was three years older and about a foot taller.

To make matters worse, Manny had been lifting weights since junior high trying to fulfill his dream of becoming a World Wrestling Federation star. In fact, Manny wouldn't play on Saturdays until the WWF TV show was finished. Unfortunately, he sometimes tried to practice some of those moves on Jimmy and Steve, despite their great resistance.

With Jim Record being a basketball nut, it wasn't long before the family added a garage with an asphalt turnaround, a perfect excuse to install a basketball hoop. Keeping it at regulation height proved challenging for Grade 5 Steve to keep up with his Grade 8 brother, but it was a challenge he enjoyed. One day while Steve was shooting baskets with his dad, Grade 6 Allison approached and asked Mr. Record if she could play. Jim was delighted to have her play because it gave him another opportunity to "coach" his beloved game.

CHAPTER 10

Smitty's Bog and the Sand Pit

The 106-acre cranberry bog behind Katydid was originally built by Alton Smith and was known as Smitty's Bog. During the early years on Katydid, the bog was owned by United Cape Cod Cranberry Associates, Inc., headed by James Hasseotes, President of Cumberland Farms. Later, Hasseotes sold the bog to the Rhodes Family Trust.

In December 2012, the United States Department of Agriculture paid the Rhodes Family Trust $1.8 million to take the bog out of cultivation. The Rhodes Family Trust then donated the bog for $1.00 to the Town of Hanson for recreational purposes, thus allowing the flora and fauna to return to their natural state.

But for the Katydid Lane kids, the bog's ownership was of little importance. For them, the bog offered many delightful hours of unsupervised play. The Scott family had a large farm abutting the bog, and for many years they provided hayrides to the public. The older rascal sleuths, knowing that Mr. Scott would take his hayride through the bog, would lay in wait at the edge of Smitty's Bog until he passed. With jackrabbit speed, they would hop aboard and enjoy the free ride. Relishing their moment of cleverness, they never realized that Mr.

Scott had been aware of their antics and generously allowed them to enjoy their free ride.

The natural beauty of the bog was particularly evident as the sun rose. Many years later, Alyce realized just how much her daughters Lauren and Deedee enjoyed its beauty. They confessed that on several occasions they would meet the older children in the neighborhood at 5:00 a.m. These nature lovers would then walk to the bogs, toting their little brown bags filled with food for a picnic breakfast that they would share. Settling themselves on the tufted grass behind the Gill's house, they would wait to see the spectacular sunrise over the bog.

The bog was more than just a place to view a beautiful sunrise. For example, the sand pit, adjacent to the bog, sparked the imagination of Katydid kids. The sand pit was a mountain of sand essential to the cultivation of cranberries. In winter, the bog company covered the plants with water. After the water froze, a layer of sand would top the ice to protect the young plants. In the spring the ice would melt, offering nutrients to the plants, and sand would cover the acidic-loving cranberries.

The kids didn't care about this at all. They just saw a ten-to-fourteen-foot mountain of sand to jump off or perilously ride their bikes down, and a snow-clad Everest to sled down in winter.

As sand eroded down the embankment, it formed a perfect jumping-off spot, and an even softer landing. The children of the lane had hours of fun jumping from the top of the embankment and rolling to the ground. Jumping off the embankment left them with the intoxicating feeling of floating in air as if they were paragliding before they fell into the cushioned arms of the soft sand. They would compete against one another to see who could jump the farthest, marking their spot and hoping to be the triumphant one, earning the title King of the Hill.

The bogs also offered walking paths. One adventure, however, brought them to the attention of the Bog Security Patrol. It started innocently enough for Jimmy aged 9, Steve aged 6, Manny aged 12, and Juan aged 11. Manny, Juan, and Steve decided to pick a few berries from the bog behind Luci's house. Because Jimmy didn't like cranberries, he waited for them in the Record yard.

Suddenly, from Route 58, a brown station wagon took a sharp right turn into the bogs, tires disrupting the gravel and creating a dirty cloud in its wake. From his perch on the hill in the backyard, Jimmy yelled, "The Bogman's here. Get out of there!"

Fleet-footed Manny took off, taking the moat between the bog and the Record's yard in one bound with Juan following closely. The younger Steve, bewildered and running as fast as he could, still lagged far behind.

Frantic, Jimmy kept shouting, "Hurry! Hurry!" as Juan cleared the moat. When Juan looked back, he saw Steve try to leap over the moat, miss, and fall in the moat surrounding the bog.

Without a moment's hesitation, Juan went back to help Steve. Now the brown station wagon was closing in on Juan and Steve. Jimmy was just above them on the hill within view of the burly man who slammed the door, exiting the car. Manny was nowhere to be found.

In a loud gruff voice, the stranger thundered, "Stop right now."

Juan could have bolted, but he stayed with Steve. The man's heavy boots crunched the grass as he approached, his face contorted and his presence towering to the youngsters. Reaching into his back pocket, the man took out a pencil and an official-looking pad. Wetting the pencil tip with his lips, he shouted, "You boys have been messing with the sprinkler system, and I'm reporting you to the police. You hoodlums belong in juvenile court. What's your names?"

A whimpering Steve, his eyes wide and watering, gave his name. Juan, trying to hide his fears, bit his lip but also gave the man his name. "What about you up there?" the bog official motioned to Jim.

"You can't coax me into telling you my name. I spent the whole time on my property."

Steve, perplexed and frightened, couldn't understand why Jimmy was talking about Cokes. "What's soda got to do with it?" he thought.

"Oh, a wise guy, are you? I certainly can take your name. Get yourself down here, right now."

"I'm staying on my property. You can't make me go into the bogs."

Frustrated after repeatedly trying to get Jimmy's name with no success, the man pointed to Juan and Steve. He taunted, "You boys gonna let him get away scot-free?"

Neither boy said a word. The man walked closer to Juan, his finger pointed menacingly. "If I see you boys again, I'll have you all arrested. Now scram, get out of here."

Steve and Juan ran as fast as they could up the hill. Terrified he was now branded with a criminal record, Steve ran immediately home and up to his room. He feared he was going to be sent to reform school.

Jimmy, on the other hand, was angry and immediately went to Steve's room. "Hey, are you crying?" he blurted as he began pacing the room. Not waiting for a response, he added, "You weren't doing anything wrong. You never touched the sprinkler system. They don't have any evidence because there isn't any. He was trying to bully you."

The more Jimmy went on, the more Steve perked up. "Yeah, you're right. He was mean."

From the doorway, Luci asked, "What's going on? You boys ran directly upstairs without stopping at the refrigerator."

As Jimmy relayed the story, growing more assertive with each detail, Luci became incensed. "Listen, you're not going to have a criminal record. He was just trying to frighten you. We'll straighten this out. Now, no more picking cranberries." The incident didn't distract them from their love of the outdoors, but it did eliminate their taste for cranberries.

In the winter, snow covered the sandpile, and that meant sledding could commence. With a variety of sleds, they would climb to the top, scream their way down, and get to the bottom eager to do it again.

The pits weren't directly visible from either Luci's or Alyce's house. Since the kids traveled as a roving "gang" led by Alyce's very able and responsible "older" girls and Jimmy, Luci's responsible oldest son, the ladies never quite realized how steep the embankment was and happily allowed them to enjoy their bog fun.

It wasn't until many years later when Luci's children were grown and brought her to the snow-covered pit that she realized that the younger children had experienced sledding adventures beyond their years. Luckily, they always returned home rosy-cheeked, smiling, and with all their limbs intact.

CHAPTER 11

Bobo

Although there were several dogs that found a home on Katydid, many of them short-lived, no dog left such a profound impression as Bobo, the Monteiro dog. A black-haired mutt who had been abused by his previous owner, Bobo was supposedly a family dog, but he favored Manny, who was the one who fed him. Always tethered by a cheap chain, Bobo often broke free.

The single greatest fear of all the children on Katydid was not that the Russians were coming, nor that a nuclear holocaust was imminent. It was the horrifying, "Bobo is loose." This fear sent kids running to their homes as fast as they could. Safety was only secured when they were behind locked doors.

One day, when Allison was seven, she tried to convince Karen to go out and play. "Come on Karen, let's ride our bikes."

Karen, comfortably ensconced in the kitchen helping her mother bake cookies, replied, "I'll go later. Mom promised that I could lick the mixer blades before the cookies go in the oven."

"Gross, wait till they come out of the oven and then you can eat them."

"No, she's letting me add the raisins to the cookies now."

"Oh, never mind, I'll go see if Steve wants to play."

Disappointed but undaunted, Allison grabbed her bike and rode up the street to the Records. Suddenly, it was too quiet on the street.

After a quick look around, she noticed Bobo was free and starting to come down the street. She thought she heard his heavy panting until she realized that *she* was the one panting.

"Can I make it to the Records? What if they don't answer the door in time?" Dropping her bike, she decided to run home instead. Bobo was already near the King's house, and he started running her way.

Never had Allison run that fast before. With Bobo gaining on her, she knew she couldn't reach the front door. When she noticed the car was in the driveway, she cut across the grass and quickly climbed onto the roof of the car. Terrified, she started to scream.

Looking out her window, Alyce saw Allison perched on top of the Buick. Quickly, she rushed outside to find Allison sobbing, her voice choking. "Bobo was chasing me."

Alyce, afraid of Bobo herself, looked up the street but did not thankfully see Bobo. She helped Allison off the car and brought her inside to soothe her with oatmeal raisin cookies and milk.

Lucky for Allison that day, Manny had whistled Bobo back. Bobo was usually chained in the side yard by the Monteiro shed, and further back was his small doghouse. He was three feet high but appeared seven feet tall to the kids.

Unfortunately, it was impossible to avoid Bobo when you played in Manny's yard. Jimmy loved sports so much that he was willing to take his chances and play baseball at the Monteiro's. The minute Jimmy arrived, the barking would begin. Fierce, tear-out-your-throat kind of barking.

This was problematic for Jimmy beyond the audio intimidation. The shed served as a backstop behind home plate to keep the ball in the playing field. Manny sometimes hit the ball hard enough that it entered the Shea's yard. Unfortunately, they never returned the ball. The worst option was that if the ball went over the backstop, it fell by Bobo.

"Hey Manny," Jimmy would casually say, "my fault for not catching that. Can you get it?" What he thought to himself was "Please God, make sure that Bobo's chain holds." He credits Bobo for encouraging him to work really hard to catch the ball and improve his baseball performance.

Even when Manny went to get the ball, it came back mauled and slobbered on with a ferocity that made Jimmy think he would clearly be dead if Bobo got to him. Although Bobo's stay on Katydid wasn't long, it left memories that haunted the children for many years.

But it wasn't only the children on Katydid that feared Bobo. Bobo was an ever-present threat to the adults as well. Alyce's greatest fear was in the mornings when the children waited in the circle for school. She always found some excuse to be at the front door or sweep her front stairs while the children waited. The neighborhood children just thought she really liked a clean front step.

Luci, on the other hand, calculated every move she made outside. Getting the mail was strategic. First, she gingerly stepped outside her front door and looked up the street like an undercover detective. If that was clear, she bolted to the mailbox, opened it, retrieved the mail, and bolted back with no unnecessary motion. She would have been a great relay runner with her quick maneuvers. Unsuspecting onlookers must have thought she was a woman with boundless energy, or someone expecting a check from Publisher's Clearinghouse.

Even the men weren't immune from intimidation from the Cujo of Katydid Lane. One weekend morning while Jim was working in the yard, the hairs on the back of his neck stood on edge. As he looked up, he saw the dreaded pit bull mix coming toward him. The dog slowly moved closer, head bent, snapping teeth bared. A snarling growl pierced the air as the canine crouched ready to attack. Jim, realizing he was defenseless, began to inch back slowly, his heart pounding, his fists clenched.

Suddenly, he heard Manny shout, "Stop, Bobo." To Jim's great relief, the dog stopped in his tracks and ambled back toward Manny. Jim slowly unclenched his fists as the tension eased.

Mustering his voice, he said to Manny, "Hey Manny, thanks for calling your dog off." It was a few minutes before Jim's heartbeat returned to normal, but he never trusted the dog again. Jim, who loves dogs, was always afraid that Bobo would run free, posing a real danger if Manny weren't around. The entire neighborhood breathed a sigh of relief when Bobo left Katydid.

CHAPTER 12

Little Women, Big Dreams

All Dressed Up and Ready for Tea

Since there were many little girls in the neighborhood, and both Alyce and Luci loved high teas, it was only natural that they would have tea parties with the girls. One especially memorable one was held in Luci's "mud room," a large, tiled room off the porch entrance.

All the girls in the neighborhood were dressed up in their prettiest dresses. Some were even in their mother's oversized dresses cinched at the waist. Hats too big for their little faces and gloves completed the ensemble for afternoon tea. Cabbage Patch kids were the rage at the time, and each of these pint-size ladies brought their chubby-faced, smartly dressed "babies" except Jill, who wanted to bring Theodore, her chipmunk doll. When Jill pulled Theodore's string, he said, "I am hungry." To this day, Jill's Theodore still announces he's hungry, a testament to the quality of old-fashioned toys.

Luci had an old jewelry box filled with costume jewelry. The youngsters immediately began to select embellishments for their outfits. Long strings of pearls adorned tiny necks. Too-big rings were taped to tiny fingers. Clip-on earrings clutched their earlobes.

Now fully bejeweled, they sat around the child-sized table festooned with colorful paper plates and napkins. Flowers and greens picked from the yard served as the centerpiece. They used Luci's mother-in-law's miniature china tea set. They drank Hawaiian punch "tea" from the tiny cups, which were soon replaced with larger paper cups, and ate peanut butter and jelly sandwiches cut in different shapes. For dessert, miniature iced cupcakes were gobbled up. Lots of giggling was heard, and frosting-covered smiles showed that the tea was a success. Hopefully, the love of high tea will be passed on to another generation.

As the women cleaned up after the tea and shared their own cups of tea, Luci remarked, "They had fun just talking and laughing together without any competition."

"And much quieter than usual," added Alyce.

"Indeed," echoed Luci. "Let's have another cup of tea."

Their reverie was interrupted when Lauren-Kate bounded down the stairs, shorts having replaced her tea party dress. "We're playing kickball in the circle. Our team against Jimmy and Steve's."

Luci looked at Alyce and said, "Oh well, our fantasy world lasted a good half hour."

Girls Got Game, 1981 Style

As Allison and Steve tossed basketballs in the Record yard, ten-year-old Steve turned to eleven-year-old Allison, "Are you going to do it?"

"Absolutely," Allison responded, her head tilting back as she corralled her raven hair behind her ear. "I'm excited."

"I can't wait to see the look on Jerry's face if you beat him," added Steve.

"What do you mean 'if' I beat him?" Allison responded.

Laughing, he spun quickly and passed the ball to her. Without hesitating, she took two steps forward, threw the ball, and into the hoop it went. Then she turned and began running to her house, shouting, "See you tomorrow."

Steve yelled back, "Don't forget to wear your best sneakers tomorrow. I'll stay after school to watch you crush Jerry."

The annual Grade 6 Free Throw contest was an important after-school ritual for sports-obsessed sixth graders at Indian Head School. The contest was open to both boys and girls; however, the consensus was it wasn't going to be much of a contest in 1981 because Jerry Johnson was the star of the Indian Head Grade 6 basketball team.

The school was abuzz with excitement. One by one the sixth graders approached the foul line and did their best, with varying degrees of success. The crowd was eagerly awaiting Jerry Johnson's turn. Jerry confidently stood on the free throw line, bounced the ball a couple of times, arched his arm, his eye on the backboard, and *swish*! Then another *swish*! He continued to make most of his attempts. Victory was within his grasp. He left the line with a big grin on his face. Subsequent contestants didn't come close to breaking his streak.

Finally, Allison approached the free-throw line. Standing behind her, Jerry and his friends shouted encouragingly, "Go Allison, take your time, you can do it," but secretly they were unsure if this pretty girl could even hit the backboard. They hoped she would get at least one in.

Much to their surprise, she did get one in, and then another, and another until the final tally revealed that she had beaten Jerry Johnson. Watching from the sidelines, Steve noticed that Jerry's grin disappeared, and a miffed expression took its place. Beaten by a girl! Oh, the humiliation for a Grade 6 boy.

Steve ran over to congratulate Allison. "You did it. I knew you could."

"I'm glad you were here to cheer me on."

During her high school years, Allison also became an accomplished 3-point shooter. Her record remained unbroken for about seven years and her accomplishment was recognized in the school trophy case. Steve was so proud of his pal. Though Steve didn't break her record, he did win the Pepsi Hot Shot Challenge in Grade 7 and Grade 8, breaking his own record. Katydid Lane was well represented among middle-school hoopsters.

The next day, Luci stopped by Alyce's after school. "Congratulations."

"For what?" questioned Alyce.

"Steve told me Allison won the free throw contest. He was so excited."

"Allison was so excited too. She practically bounced home that day. I was so proud of her. Basketball certainly has changed since I played CYO basketball. Girls could only go half court."

"Did they think we would faint traveling those extra yards?" Luci said, melodramatically fanning herself.

Alyce continued to reminisce. "Remember when guards had to be on one side of the court and the forwards had to be on the other side of the court? If you were a guard, you could never score."

"Not much of an incentive to practice dribbling and stealing the ball if you were a guard," argued Luci. "Do you realize, Alyce, what an accomplishment it is to compete on the same level as boys? When *we* were in school, they relegated us to cheering from the sidelines. Heaven help us if we ever bruised a boy's ego by beating him in sports. I guess we should be grateful they passed the 19th Amendment. We should smile and just look pretty," she mocked, batting her eyelashes.

"Well, I don't feel pretty folding these clothes. Put the teapot on and I'll throw in another load of clothes."

Alice in Wonderland

One summer day on Katydid Lane, the children delighted their parents with a production of Lewis Carroll's *Through the Looking Glass* and *What Alice Found There*. Maura Gill directed the production. The characters were Jill Hennelly as Alice, Blair Gill as the soloist, Lauren-Kate Record as Tweedledee, Amy Shea as Tweedledum, Teddy Madison as the Mad Hatter, and Joey Shea as the stage manager.

At the Gill house, director Maura was facing stiff opposition from her sister Blair.

"How come I can't be Alice?" pleaded Blair.

"Because I'm the director. You're such a little pest. I made you the soloist, didn't I?" countered Maura as she picked up the script and began walking to her room. "If you keep asking, I'll give the part to someone else, and you can just pass out programs," she chortled. "The director makes the decisions."

Undaunted, Blair quickly followed her saying, "Jill doesn't even want to be Alice. She hates wearing that blue dress."

"She never told me that so I'm not changing my mind. Go practice your song."

"Ooh, you are so bossy," Blair thought as she grabbed her song sheet and stomped out of the room. "I'm going to be the best soloist ever," she promised herself. Oh, the compromises that younger siblings face in the shadow of older siblings.

Blair's assessment of Jill's lack of enthusiasm to wear the blue satin dress was accurate, and it took some convincing on Alyce's part.

"You have an important part in the play, Jill. Alice can't be in pants. It'll be fine. It's just one performance."

"I look silly in it. It makes noise when I walk. I might even forget my lines with all the noise. All those ruffles, ugh!"

Despite a couple of dramatic distractions, the cast settled into their roles, and for weeks, the children rushed home after swim practice each day to rehearse their parts. Learning their lines, assembling their props, and deciding on costumes occupied them for hours on end.

Finally, opening day arrived. Nature set the stage with a beautiful summer afternoon. The play was performed on the Gill's backyard deck. Chairs were neatly arranged for the audience of mothers to view the performance. The girls even distributed programs.

Comfortably ensconced in their seats, the moms were an enthusiastic audience, relishing the creativity of their young thespians. Cameras clicked at regular intervals capturing one scene after another.

Suddenly, with no discernible explanation, Maura interrupted the performance momentarily when Blair began to sing, much to Blair's embarrassment. Quite the trooper, Blair quickly recovered and continued singing beautifully.

Teddy, the only male character in the play, delivered his two Mad Hatter lines, "Did not, did not" brilliantly. After taking final bows, these actors giggled and hugged each other, and quickly left the "stage."

As they were leaving the stage, Maura whispered to Blair, "You did a great job as a soloist." Blair just beamed. They returned with trays of lemonade and cookies they had made and began serving the audience. All enjoyed the creative production in their little "theater" on Katydid Lane.

Beautiful Girl in the House

On the rare occasions that Luci and Jim went out, the issue of finding babysitters was paramount. Thankfully, Alyce had two older girls who could babysit. The dilemma was that when Jim was eleven, he thought he was old enough to babysit, claiming he "wasn't a baby."

Giving Jimmy total authority as the babysitter was an idea Steve opposed, listing his grievances in detail. He exclaimed vociferously, "I don't want him to babysit. He thinks he's the boss of the family. He won't let me do *anything*." Because Steve was only eight and Lauren-Kate only five, Luci agreed with Steve.

After the children were adults, they shared harrowing stories of their adventures when Jimmy was later left to babysit. Luci and Jim gasped in horror. Stories of baseball games in the family room that left the front window broken were explained as "accidents." Lauren-Kate shared that the boys would spin her around by her legs in the family room so close to the fireplace hearth that she was terrified. These stories were belated confirmation that their earlier decision to hire babysitters was a good one.

On one occasion, Deedee, a mature fourteen, was hired to babysit. When Jimmy complained to Manny and Juan that Deedee would be babysitting that Saturday, they were jealous. "She's beautiful, and she'll be at your house for hours. Lucky."

Jimmy was conflicted. He didn't want a babysitter, but Manny and Juan thought it was good to have a beautiful girl in his house. The situation was very confusing to a preadolescent young boy who was still processing this conundrum. But it wasn't confusing to Manny.

First, he began circling the house that night. Finally mustering up some courage, he rang the doorbell. Deedee looked out the window before answering the door. Manny, smiling broadly, his hands nervously in his pockets, pretended to be surprised when Deedee answered the door.

"Hey, Dee, what are you doing here? I just came over to see if Jimmy wanted to play a little b-ball."

"Manny, I'm here because Mr. and Mrs. Record went out. Sorry, you can't come in and Jimmy can't go out. I just made some popcorn, and we are just going to watch a movie. See you tomorrow," she said and gently closed the door.

Manny headed down the stairs, shaking his head. Images of sitting on the sofa watching a movie floated in his head. That fantasy bubble burst, and he reluctantly got on his bike and circled the Record driveway one more time before pedaling home, defeated in his attempt to get Deedee's attention.

The Girls Fight Muscular Dystrophy

During the 60s and 70s the Muscular Dystrophy Association, promoted by comedian Jerry Lewis, included a way for children to help raise money for Jerry's Kids by having backyard carnivals. When Lauren Hennelly was eleven, she was determined to help. She found that Deedee and her friend Katy were eager to help. They quickly sent away for the packet from the organization that would turn their next month into an exciting time of planning and preparing for their fundraiser.

The packet arrived filled with ideas, props, and tickets, including typed fortunes to be used at a fortune teller's booth. Lots of work had to be done. First, the where and when needed to be determined. With Katy's four older brothers a source of constant teasing, their yard was immediately eliminated. The girls decided the carnival would be held in the Hennelly's backyard because the girls were always there anyway.

Parts and "booths" had to be assigned. Katy was chosen to be the soothsayer and Deedee would be the clown who would entertain the babies. "Katy," said Lauren, "my mom has a long flowing skirt with a draped top that would be perfect. Do you have any colorful scarves?"

"Not me, but my mom does. I'll ask." Lightweight, colorful scarves would adorn her head, shoulders, and waist. Lots of bracelets and a pair of hooped earrings would finish the outfit, and Katy would be transformed into a real fortune teller.

Lauren turned to Deedee. "Why don't you wear that Halloween costume you wore last October?"

"Good idea Lauren. I don't know where it is, but I know Mom would have kept it. Let's ask her." After a quick yell into the kitchen, within minutes the costume appeared. There it was: a pink satin clown suit with three white pompoms. A dunce-like pink satin hat topped with a big white pompom covered her blond braids. With big lipstick-red apple cheeks and a tiny lipstick-tipped nose, Deedee was ready. With that settled, they started planning the carnival.

The girls spent weeks making a fortune teller's booth out of cardboard boxes. After several days of collecting boxes from BPM, the local market, these entrepreneurs began the task of changing cartons of Charmin toilet paper and towels into a proper booth. Dulling many pairs of scissors, they cut and duct-taped the cartons together. As black paint obscured the labels, Charmin became a charming booth. But they wanted more. The ideas then began to flow.

"I've got an idea for the older children," Lauren piped up. An egg-on-a-spoon race, a water balloon toss, a rocking horse ride, and ring toss games were added.

"Maybe selling candy bars, having a bake sale, and selling cold drinks would make it feel like a real carnival," Deedee added. Cupcakes were baked and frosted, cookies were made, and candy bars were bought for the upcoming event.

The day of the carnival approached quickly. Time to sell advance tickets to the neighbors. The girls ran from door to door with flyers announcing the upcoming carnival. As usual, the turnout and support from the neighbors was heartwarming, and everyone purchased admission tickets and vowed to come.

The Hennelly's yard had colorful banners and balloons strewn throughout, creating a festive atmosphere. The fortune teller's booth was popular among the children. They could walk up to the booth, pick a typed fortune from a jar, and see what their futures held. The bake sale table was a delight for all their sugar-loving friends, and the rocking horse ride had a long line of little ones waiting for their turn. The children who were unsuccessful at the water balloon toss were easily identified, for they all walked around with wet T-shirts. The weather cooperated and everyone had fun at the carnival.

Not a lot of money was raised, fifteen to twenty dollars tops, but the children were excited with their small donation and overjoyed when they received a thank you letter from Jerry Lewis himself.

PART II

The Improvement Phase: Tune Up Time for Mind, Body, and Soul

CHAPTER 13

Battling Time and Gravity

Dieting was an ever-present issue in our gals' lives. Through out the years, they tried many ways to maintain their weight. Incentives were the key to a lasting effort, and exercising was an essential component of weight loss. Rewarding themselves with prizes and paying money to the person who lost the most weight was the most successful tactic.

To be honest, they were never candidates for the Biggest Loser show, but both wanted to be at a healthy weight as they aged. Before Luci went back to work in 1979, Luci and Alyce found excuses to see each other every day, but always, in their words, "with a purpose." No idle get-togethers just sipping tea and eating bonbons, though they did find plenty of time to taste new recipes.

On this day, Luci argued, "Alyce, it's time to bite the bullet. Little steps aren't working. We must face the reality that if we don't do something, we'll slide into sloth. We have to shame ourselves into losing weight."

"Oh, no. What hare-brained idea are you proposing?" Alyce asked.

"We must dress in our tightest outfits and take photos—front, side, and rear views. They'll be so awful it will motivate us to stop the feeding frenzy."

"We can't show these photos to anyone."

"Are you crazy? Who would want to?"

The next day, with their Polaroids ready, they took clandestine blackmail-worthy shots. To be more cringeworthy, Luci even slouched. It worked. This became one of their most successful techniques. Alyce says she's been plagued by those photos for over thirty years. Thank goodness this was before smartphones, the internet, and viral videos. Luci found it easier just to throw the pictures away.

Another incentive that was less damaging to their psyche was rewarding themselves by purchasing any item they wanted after they lost the requisite weight. Alyce still has a beautiful white nightgown in her lingerie drawer marking her first weight loss win.

One time she convinced her sister-in-law Ruthie and her friend Jane to participate in a Lose Weight Challenge. Everyone would put in money and the one who lost the most would win all the loot. Now *this* was a competition that Luci could commit to. A win-win situation, as she won the money and lost the weight.

Weight wasn't the only focus of these health nuts. Facials were important to maintain a radiant complexion but were too expensive for these young mothers. What to do? They would make their own facials. To the supermarket they went to purchase avocados. They had oatmeal in the house, so they gathered in Alyce's big kitchen to prepare a concoction of avocado and oatmeal and apply it to their faces.

Of course, they didn't just sit serenely in lounge chairs, listening to classical music with eucalyptus wafting through the air. They sat on Alyce's kitchen benches, chatting the whole time with the aroma from Alyce's dutch-oven supper simmering away on the stove. Alyce manned the blender, adding the oatmeal until a siren-like whirr signaled it was ready.

Meanwhile, Luci was at the table with the avocado poised expertly in her left hand. After slicing the avocado, she quickly karate-chopped the pit and out it came. "Okay Alyce, ready to mash." Within minutes the mixture was ready.

"I'll get towels, so we won't get it on our clothes," cautioned Alyce.

"We're wearing sweatshirts, Alyce. It probably won't matter."

"Okay."

They pulled their hair away from their faces and slathered on the green concoction. With their short, dark hair framing their faces, they were a cross between the Jolly Green Giant and the Hulk. Now all they had to do was wait twenty minutes for the mixture to work its magic.

"Can you imagine what our friends would say, Alyce, if they saw us now?"

"They'd be green with envy."

"Don't make me laugh. I'll have to add more mix so it won't fall off."

"It's healthy, so if it slides off, we can eat it."

Miraculously, it stayed on for the whole twenty minutes, but when they rinsed it off, they were still their jolly selves with no dramatic change in their complexions.

The next week, they were determined to try an egg-white facial. When Alyce arrived at Luci's, Luci had already prepared the egg whites.

"Alyce, I have these at room temperature because I know that when we bake, they always tell us to use room-temperature eggs."

"But Luci, we're not baking this facial, so we could have used them straight out of the refrigerator."

"The directions say to whip it a bit, but I don't want to make meringue, so we can lightly whip it with a fork," said Luci.

While Luci was talking, Alyce had already whipped her egg white and applied it to her face. Luci quickly followed suit. Within minutes, Luci wanted to offer Alyce tea, but what came out was garbled. As the mixture dried and their faces became stiff with dried egg whites, they found it very hard to talk. What a failure. Fifteen minutes of silence and no tea. Unacceptable. They never tried that one again.

On another occasion, they tried facial exercises. "Luci, just pucker your lips and rotate them thirty times in one direction and thirty times in the opposite direction. It will ward off wrinkles and sagging skin."

"That sounds counterintuitive. Wouldn't all that rotating increase wrinkles?" argued Luci.

"Well, I just read it in a magazine. It's supposed to build your facial muscles. Anyway, I have another tip. Frown and then open your eyes as wide as possible to the count of fifteen."

"Alyce, all this is doing is giving me a headache."

"Well, Luci, when I'm eighty and looking good, you will be sorry you didn't try these tips."

"I'll live on the wild side and take my chances. Mother Nature is cruel, Alyce, and always wins out in the end."

Because homemade facials didn't produce the desired results, they tried to tackle frizzy hair instead. By now, the ladies had let their hair grow longer and had been fighting the frizz all summer. As fall brought cooler days and children in school, it was time to really attack the problem.

With towel in one hand and Hellman's mayonnaise in the other, Luci walked over to Alyce's one bright Tuesday morning. "I'm here, ready to transform my hair into smooth, cascading locks."

"I'll wet your hair over the sink, and then you can wet mine."

They towel-dried their hair before applying the mayonnaise and then covered their hair with shower caps.

"You know, Alyce, some people would think we're crazy, but mayo is egg, oil, and vinegar. So that's protein, and vinegar makes hair shine. I think we're on to something."

"It's a lot cheaper than what those fancy spas charge for hair treatments. We don't even have to drive anywhere or get dressed up. Plus, I made a coffee cake."

For the next half hour, they sat with mayonnaise-covered hair eating coffee cake and sipping tea and smelling like a baloney sandwich.

Back home after her shower, Luci called Alyce, "How does your hair look?"

"Very soft and shiny."

"Me too. I've always liked Hellman's."

Through the years, they continued to have so much fun experimenting. To this day they both look darn good for their age. For them, their philosophy has been not to deny aging, but never to give up trying to improve their mind, body, and spirit.

CHAPTER 14

Let's Get Physical

Fencing Foils

Fencing seems like an unusual way to lose weight; however, for our thirty-something women, it was perfectly normal. One day while Luci was cleaning her attic, she found two fencing foils that Jim's Aunt Tre had left him. The foils, called épées, had triangular cross-sectioned blades. Before getting together to exercise that day, Luci called Alyce. "Alyce, I'm bringing over two fencing swords we can use instead of the Jane Fonda tape."

"What kind of exercises can we do with them?" asked Alyce.

"Lunges, maybe some arm work."

Not convinced, Alyce asked, "Does it come with instructions?"

"No, but we've seen enough Errol Flynn swashbuckling movies to know what they do. Besides, I've never seen a fat fencer," assured Luci.

"What fencer have you seen?"

"Errol Flynn. It'll be fun."

Now convinced, Alyce replied, "I'm game."

When Alyce opened the door, she saw Luci standing holding two weapons over three feet long.

"Those look dangerous," Alyce worried.

"Try not to go for the heart. Seriously, we won't actually make contact."

Alyce was still not convinced. "Don't they wear protective headgear and pads?"

Luci laughed, "Oh, Alyce. That's in competition. We're only going to exercise."

"Let's create a routine, like five steps forward, five steps backward, lunging on forward. Then we can cross swords to work the arms," suggested Alyce.

"That sounds good. We should get in position. We have to raise one arm up and over the shoulder like they do on TV. Our knees have to be bent a bit." Luci demonstrated.

Armed with only two fencing words, "en garde" and "touché," our ladies raised weapons in the air, took the fencing stance, and began exercising. To an observer, it probably looked more like an attack.

They pranced around Alyce's kitchen like Errol Flynn hoping to burn off a few calories with total disregard for the dangers of wielding untipped blades. When Luci's blade came dangerously close to the kitchen ceiling, she said nervously, "Wait, we may want to rethink what we're doing. It's not safe."

"Well, we did get a little exercise and we had plenty of laughs. Imagine if someone were looking in the window. Luci, we look insane."

This gave way to more laughter and giggles than any real weight loss benefit. In fact, if laughter were a weight loss solution, these two would be super-slim models.

Ballet Blues

Trying to obtain beauty in motion as a goal toward weight loss, these two adventurers decided that perhaps ballet would give them the graceful movement that would slough off weight, maintain good posture, and enable them to express themselves on the dance floor.

Dancing lessons were not new to Luci after taking years of tap dancing when she was younger. Her mother wanted all three of her girls to be "well rounded" but Luci's love of food, an obsession she possessed naturally, made Luci herself the only thing "well rounded."

Unlike Luci, Alyce was a novice to dance, but the idea was intoxicating. Off to the local dance studio in Marshfield for adult ballet class they went. Excited and giddy, they signed up for a five-week course.

They anticipated women with their hair in tight buns, their tiny feet in ballet slippers, and their bodies pencil thin. That was not what these forty-year-olds saw. "See Alyce," Luci whispered, "we can do this. They look normal."

Indeed, the group of about ten women varied in age—most in their thirties and forties— and body types, from thin to "pleasantly plump." Dressed in leotards, these quasi-ballerinas pirouetted, plied, and arabesqued around the studio while the two newcomers in sweats valiantly tried to keep up.

Alyce was questioning her abilities once she realized she was always at the end of the line. "Could it be," she thought, "because I'm the shortest?" Looking around the room, she realized there were shorter people in the class, including Luci. Turning to Luci, she sighed and said, "Oh goodness, Luci, they keep putting me last because I'm the worst."

"Not so," reassured Luci. "It's because we are new."

At the same time, Luci looked into the room-wide mirror and thought, "This is hysterical! We look ridiculous! The whole group looks ridiculous." For the rest of the class, Luci battled to maintain her composure, her muscles tensing as she tried not to burst out laughing. One by one, they had to cross the room, twirling with their arms over their heads.

The urge to laugh became so great that she started coughing to hold back the laughter. Before long, they decided that maybe their ballet days had passed them by.

Wet and Wild

In 1985 Alyce and Ron installed a pool in their backyard and the opportunity arose for a different kind of exercise. Luci was interested but apprehensive.

"But I can't swim, Alyce."

"Okay. We'll start off in the shallow end and do water aerobics for about twenty minutes. When you're relaxed, we'll venture out into the deep end, and we'll use Clorox bottles. I'll empty the bottles and you can hold onto them. You'll float. That'll do it. We need buoyancy and resistance," Alyce said with confidence.

Readers may wonder why Alyce would have two full bottles of Clorox ready to empty, but with five active daughters, the answer is clear. Into a big bucket she poured the Clorox and returned with two empty bottles. "Okay, Luci. Use these."

"How am I going to use my arms if they're holding the bottles?"

"The bottles are for the deep end. Now we'll be exercising in the shallow end."

"Can't we do everything in the shallow end?"

"No, some of the exercises won't work there. The bottles will help you to stay in a horizontal position at the surface of the water. You'll be able to float and kick your legs."

"A horizontal position? I don't want to reenact the dead man's float," countered Luci.

"Don't worry. I'll be right with you. I haven't lost a swimmer yet," laughed Alyce.

"Okay, but if I drown, it'll be your fault."

"One more thing. I'll be right back," said Alyce as she rushed into the garage and emerged with a boombox over her shoulder. "This will set the mood," she said as she pressed play. Rod Stewart began to croon, "Forever Young."

In one quick motion, Alyce dove into the pool. "Come on Luci. Your turn."

Armed with her new swimming apparatus, Luci timidly entered the water.

"Alyce, these Clorox bottles are emitting fumes. I'd better do something quickly before I faint," she said as she feigned swooning.

"Okay, stop making excuses."

"You're such a tyrant," laughed Luci.

Exercising in the shallow end went very well until Alyce uttered those frightening words, "Grab the Clorox and walk into the deep end."

Taking a deep breath, Luci inched forward, tiptoeing into the deep end while clutching the Clorox bottles.

"Keep coming," urged Alyce.

Suddenly Luci's toes did not touch the pool bottom. "Yikes, I'm over my head."

"That's the idea. Now lift your legs up and kick," instructed Alyce.

Luci tried to lift her legs, but they felt like cement blocks. "It's not working. They won't go up."

"Okay, I'll try to help." Alyce dove under and grabbed Luci's right leg. Luci's head immediately fell back into the water. Her arms began flailing and the Clorox bottles bobbed away. "*Stop*," screamed Luci. "I'm drowning."

Alyce, fearing a swift right-leg kick was imminent, quickly released Luci's leg. "Don't panic. Grab my arm and I'll bring you to the side."

Coughing and shaking her water-soaked head, Luci immediately grabbed Alyce's arm as safety was just a few feet away.

Alyce did a lot of laundry that week, and Ron's t-shirts were never whiter. Luci, however, has had an aversion to Clorox ever since.

The Gym

As Luci and Alyce were walking one day, Luci mused, "We do a lot of walking for exercise, which is good, but we're not getting any younger. Maybe we should join a gym to get back in shape. Like for tennis."

"We were never in tennis shape," said Alyce.

"We could build up our stamina."

"Why are we joining a gym to improve our tennis? Shouldn't we take tennis lessons instead?" countered Alyce.

"We're not doing it for tennis. We need to build up more muscle strength."

"Well, you're right, and Gold's Gym is right down the street. We can take a tour, try out the equipment, and decide if we want to be members," said Alyce enthusiastically.

Who would have expected that when signing up for a membership at Gold's Gym, Alyce would meet her future son-in-law? Their trainer was a young man known as Clubber. He was patient, knowledgeable, and the perfect spokesperson to represent the gym. After instructing the women on which machines would be the most beneficial for them, he left them to their own devices. His instructions were to complete fifteen reps five times on one machine before going to the next machine.

However, the ladies misinterpreted his instructions. After doing fifteen reps on the weight machine, they did fifteen reps on the ab machine, followed by fifteen reps on the leg machine. Once finished with the three machines, they began the cycle all over again to complete their five rotations.

Clubber, or Bobby, as the women would later call him, noticed lots of movement between the women and checked in to see how they were doing.

"Ladies, I noticed you were moving around the gym a lot."

"Yeah! Aren't you impressed? We've done all the exercises and we haven't collapsed," said Luci.

"That's good, but I wanted you to stay on one machine and complete the fifteen reps five times before moving on to really work the muscles."

"Oh, sorry," said Alyce. "We'll follow directions better the next time."

"You ladies are doing great. Keep up the good work," encouraged Bobby as he left.

Now on the treadmill, Luci turned to Alyce. "Alyce, while the treadmill allows us to chat, it's boring. In fact, all the machines are boring. Did you see that they offer aerobic classes? Exercising to music sounds so much better."

"Whew, I find the machines boring, too. Let's quit these machines and go upstairs and see if they're having an aerobics class now," agreed Alyce.

"Sounds like a plan," said Luci.

Even from the stairs, the deep bass of the music reverberated. They looked at each other and said, "Way more fun than the machines."

As they were signing up, they noticed the racquetball courts.

Racquetball became their go-to game. Surprisingly, they were evenly matched and competitive. They worked on their game and played for an hour at a time. However, as the game waned in popularity, the gym reduced the number of courts and they had fewer opportunities to play.

Rollerblading

In their sixties, these fitness aficionados wanted to try rollerblading, a popular activity at the time. One fall day as they sat having tea at Alyce's, Alyce remarked, "Luci, Allison and the girls have started rollerblading and they love it. You can really build up a sweat. They have all the equipment. We could rollerblade in Plymouth and head to the Cape Cod Canal, and best of all, it wouldn't cost us anything."

That "best of all" caught Luci's attention. Although she was a bit apprehensive, she was willing to face her fears.

"Great," said Alyce. "I'll call Allison and we can borrow her stuff."

This was Luci's biggest fear: Alyce's uncanny ability to get things done. She had hoped her reluctant enthusiasm would stall this adventure and perhaps even derail it. No such luck.

A quick call to Allison followed by a quicker trip to Allison's house and they were on their way to Plymouth. This decision was made possible because they were always dressed for exercise. The days of *Leave It To Beaver's* June Cleaver were over. In that popular late 50s and 60s sitcom, the wife, June, was a stay-at-home wife who was always attired in fashionable dresses that were partially covered by equally attractive aprons as she did her daily chores. Never seen cleaning the toilet, moving furniture, or changing a tire, June was not the model these gals aspired to emulate.

They headed down to Plymouth and the Cape Cod Canal where there was a seven-mile paved path. Safe from motor vehicles and curbs, these rollerbladers donned their blades and knee guards and attempted to coast along.

Well, for Luci, that was not happening. It was more like making it from one post to another as she grasped for dear life. All Alyce could hear was, "Ooh, no eeeeno, ooh" then two quick Hulk-like forward steps, followed by an "Oh, God." Luci was ready to take off her blades, convinced a hip injury was in her future, or worse. Traumatized, she wanted to keep her knee pads on because even with the blades off, her legs were so wobbly.

"You're a good sport for trying, Luci. Let's put this stuff away and go get lunch," said Alyce. Music to Luci's ears.

Pins Drop And So Does Luci

In their early seventies, Luci suggested they return to bowling, a sport they had done in the past. Bowling seemed like a fairly simple sport. Off they went to Hanover's Boston Bowl, now a fancy upgrade from their earlier days at the Hanson Bowladrone. This alley included high-end equipment and everything was automated, including scoring.

Since this was a Tuesday and school was in session, there were very few people there. First, they had to sign in and decide whether to rent bowling shoes. It was an easy decision for Alyce, who was wearing sandals.

Luci, on the other hand, was wearing sneakers, so she figured, "Why spend five dollars renting bowling shoes?" Boston Bowl did include the incentive of a brand-new pair of socks with the rental. She had plenty of socks, so sneakers it was.

Now at their assigned alley with the scoring sheet displayed on the screen above, they were ready. Luci was the first one up. Cradling a bowling ball in her hands, she took three steps back, aligned herself with the alley, and one, two, three! Her legs propelled her forward, but her sneakers held her back and she face-planted on the bowling alley floor.

Her dear friend Alyce was in spasms laughing and didn't respond quickly to this perilous situation until after Luci slowly picked herself up. They checked for broken bones and missing teeth. Thankfully, Luci was still intact, except for a bruised ego. She quickly changed into bowling shoes, the $5.00 well spent because her performance improved immensely.

Perky Peddlers

From all these experiences, it would appear that Luci had been cloistered as a child, but as a young girl, she really did prefer being in the house reading and spending time with her grandmother. Luci did, however, learn to ride a bike as a child. At eight she received a beautiful powder-blue Huffy bike for Christmas, which she rode often.

Those were the days when you controlled a bike with the pedals, making it very easy to stop. There were no multiple gears to worry about, and a girl bike's top bar was so low that it was easy to get on and off without injuring any part of the human anatomy. The problem was that Luci didn't maintain this skill when new bikes introduced gears, hand shifts, and higher bars across the top.

A sucker for punishment, Luci offered little resistance when Alyce suggested biking.

"Do you think bike riding in our seventies is safe?" Luci questioned.

"Oh course, haven't you been riding that stationary bike you got at the yard sale?"

"Which stationary bike, Alyce? I've bought two at yard sales already and I never use either of them. You know what a parsimonious optimist I am. They were practically giving them away at the yard sale, and I kept hoping I'd become inspired if they were in the house. Maybe I'll buy a new bike."

However, Luci's new bike didn't immediately make biking an easy experience. As Alyce jaunted along, legs gracefully moving in a fluid motion and hands expertly balanced, she took a deep breath and said, "The best of biking for me is the freedom and a sense of adventure."

Luci trudged behind, hands white-knuckled on the handlebars and body uncomfortably balanced on the hard, too-high seat. She retorted, "Freedom is not what I feel. I'm feeling stressed, and I'm praying that other riders will pass me quickly and oncoming riders will avoid me and move right. My adventure is finding streets so I can walk the bike across."

"Can't you enjoy the beautiful floral scents as we ride the trail?"

"I hate to break it to you, Alyce, but the scent's the same when you walk the trail."

"Oh Luci, think positively."

"I'm positive that I can enjoy nature on two feet," she said.

Eventually, Luci became more comfortable, and riding became easier. She even came to enjoy the seasonal changes that riding in New England provides. Over time, they biked Wampatuck Park in Hingham, the Cape Cod Canal, and the Falmouth bike trail, all with little or no mishaps to themselves.

The Road Runners

Alyce took up running in her early fifties and had run many races. Her favorite competition was the 10K. Her first 10k race was the Bonnie Bell Woman's Race in Boston, which she ran with her daughter Jill. She went on to run four half-marathons in Miami in addition to the Boston Marathon, which she ran in 2006 with her daughters Allison and Jill and Gretchen, a family friend.

But during that period, she could never convince Luci to join her. Now both in their seventies and retired, she tried again.

"Luci, you're always running to the mailbox or running down to my house, and you practically race through the supermarket. Why not try running a couple of miles with me?"

"A couple of miles? I'm a purposeful runner: getting mail or doing shopping. Running just to run is boring. I'd rather play a game for exercise. I'm exhausted watching you run. But I don't mind running up and down Katydid or even running to Shaws and back."

"Well, that's a start. I'll stop by tomorrow and we can run to Shaws."

"Perfect, I'm making a cake and I need sour cream."

"That's great that you need something that needs refrigeration. That'll force you to keep a steady pace before the sour cream lives up to its name," added Alyce.

Luci never developed a passion for running, but she saw how much Alyce enjoyed it and how her own children did, especially Stephen and Lauren-Kate. Stephen ran on Thayer Academy's Cross-Country team that won the Independent League State Championship and he also ran Falmouth Road Race. Lauren-Kate and Steve both ran in triathlons. Luci wanted to experience that "runner's high," and more importantly share in the camaraderie after the race with the other runners enjoying donuts and energy bars.

Luci ran her first race with her daughter Lauren-Kate and Lauren-Kate's boys in the Hanover Turkey Trot. At the time the boys were seven, nine, and ten. The day was brisk, perfect for running, and Luci was eager to finally be at the finish line as a runner, not an observer. To bask in after-race euphoria sounded so tempting.

However, the beginning of the race was the only time Luci saw

Lauren-Kate and the boys until they greeted her at the finish line. She couldn't even outrun the seven-year-old Chris. But she didn't give up. She entered the Moving Heels for Meals on Wheels, a 5K race held on April 2, 2017. Luci took first place in her division, her first 5K race, and received a medal that she proudly displays.

Of course, to be fair, the division was seventy and older and Luci only had to beat three other oldsters. When telling Alyce about the race, she omitted the number of division competitors. "A win is a win," she convinced herself.

Recently, Alyce ran Warrior Dash in New York with her family and the Spartan Race in Bethel Woods with her daughter Jill, her granddaughter Mikayla, and her grandson Zachary.

For Alyce, running has become a passion, and she continues to run to this day. For Luci, she continues to run to the mailbox.

CHAPTER 15

Teaching Old Dogs New Tricks

A Night With Monet

When Luci's daughter-in-law Chrissy, naturally artistic, showed her a painting she had created at a wine and painting party, Luci was very impressed. "It's easy," gushed Chrissy. "The professional artist is there to tell you what brushes to use." It took no convincing to get Alyce on board. They signed up immediately and drove the hour-long ride to Natick the next Tuesday evening, all excited to discover their untapped artistic talent.

Entering the studio, they noticed stations set up so each "artist" had her own easel, brushes, paints, and apron. In the center of the room, a small buffet table was filled with water, wine, and small appetizers. The instructor's station was in the front of the room. She began by offering a glass of wine and appetizers to anyone who wanted to indulge. Our budding Picassos, of course, wanted the total experience, so they accepted the wine and appetizers. Luci whispered to Alyce, "My classes never started like this before."

"Well," agreed Alyce, "This certainly takes all the stress out of schoolwork."

The assignment was to replicate Monet's *Water Lilies*. How hard could it be to reproduce one of the greatest impressionist paintings? Undaunted, they charged headlong into transforming their blank canvases into masterpieces. Brushstroke by brushstroke, the instructor would announce which paintbrush to use, and then demonstrate how to create that stroke. For Luci, just getting the right brush and creating the right swish or dab or sweep proved challenging.

"My bridge doesn't look right, Alyce. It doesn't seem in proportion to the lilies."

"You're too critical. No one's going to think our paintings are so good that we could become art forgers. We're doing this for fun."

"You're right, although my dreams of creating a masterpiece are dashed," she laughed.

In the end, Alyce was able to do a respectable job and displayed her painting, but Luci, still critical of her attempt, soon relegated her painting to the attic. Monet's reputation as the master was secure. It did spark an interest in both of them, though. Alyce later began water-coloring, and Luci created a few canvasses to decorate her home.

The success of the evening was not in the painting itself but in another opportunity to laugh and try something new. Thankfully, the class was long enough and their wine glasses small enough that they remained clear-headed to drive home, but there did seem to be even more laughter than usual that night.

Speed Reading

In another attempt to improve themselves, these middle-aged scholars forayed into the world of education by taking an evening class at Maquan Elementary School in Hanson. Mrs. Lewis, the music teacher at the elementary and middle school, had a son who was offering a speed-reading class. "How interesting," said Alyce when Luci mentioned that this might be something they might like to do. Off they went to sign themselves up and take their first class.

The room was filled with approximately twenty adults of varying ages. To assist his students in increasing their reading speed as well as their comprehension, their instructor began by suggesting to the students that while reading, they might skip over such words as "and, but, the, then" and any other word that connected the sentence.

Their assignment was to read a paragraph or two and then answer questions to make sure they were comprehending the topic. As soon as they were finished, they were to approach the teacher's desk. The teacher would then correct the paper and note the time and the grade on their paper. "This way," he noted, "you can track your improvement."

An air of expectancy arose as the teacher passed out the first reading. "Keep this face down, please, until I give the signal." You would have thought these were state secrets not to be divulged until instructed. Slowly, he returned to his desk, sat down, picked up his stopwatch, and announced with great solemnity, "Begin."

Luci was a star. Within a few minutes of getting the assignment, Luci was at the instructor's desk, the first one in the class to finish and always with one hundred percent comprehension. Taking the instructor's suggestion, Alyce was at her desk trying to eliminate "and, but, the, then" and any other word that connected the sentence and could only watch in amazement as Luci aced that class.

Majoring in Cooking and Coding

Not content with self-taught classes, these lifelong learners decided to actually take adult education evening courses offered at Brockton High School. What a vast array of choices at their disposal. But which choice should they make?

Alyce selected her choice right away: Medical Transcribing. She could add the very practical course to her resume on the chance that she might return to the workforce one day.

On the other hand, Luci wavered. Should she sign up for upholstery so she could redo her wing chair, or try yoga to get in shape? And then she spotted it: Authentic Italian Cooking with Mrs. San Martino. Their selections were on the same day and at the same time but in separate classrooms. Big mistake on Alyce's part. While Alyce's course was more cerebral, Luci's was much more fun and a gustatory treat each week.

This was the first course Mrs. San Martino had taught, so she went all out. Each week there was a different theme. She assigned the students to different stations. As Mrs. San Martino made the dish, the class would also make the dish. After the dishes were made, the students gathered at tables and enjoyed the fruits of their labor.

When they met after class in the parking lot, Alyce would notice how an aroma surrounded Luci. "Oh, what did you make tonight, Luci?" Alyce groaned, rubbing her tired right hand from notetaking.

Each week Luci gushed to Alyce about all the new recipes she was making, from Italian rum cake to arancini. "Alyce, you have to taste the arancini. I'll buy the ingredients and we can make it together."

Before the next class, Alyce and Luci made the arancini: a rice ball filled with meat and cheese, then covered in crumbs and deep fried. Although it called for many steps, two cooks made the job easier. Encasing a ground meat and pea mixture in starchy, cheesy rice, then covering it in crumbs and deep frying it may not sound appetizing, but it was delicious, and Alyce loved it.

Arancini became a recipe they would continue to make to the delight of their families. However, Alyce had lists and lists of medical terms that she would never use. She could hardly wait for that class to be over.

PART III

The Project Phase: Getting Crafty

CHAPTER 16

Pins and Needles and Other Handiwork

Stained Glass

For our intrepid crafters, the more inexperienced they were in the craft, the more interesting it became to tackle. Take stained glass, for instance. Both admired the classic beauty of stained-glass windows, especially the ones they had seen on a recent house tour. As they left the house, they simultaneously looked at each other and knew they had found their next project.

What a learning experience. They weren't ready to tackle real glass, so they found colored plastic that melted to replicate real glass. Next, they bought the lead to frame and support the plastic. They quickly learned that there were different sizes and channels of lead. Armed with this knowledge, they had to learn to solder.

At first, they wondered if they would have to get hard hats and welding torches to complete their projects. The thought was terrifying. These ladies were smart but not crazy. Two women who laugh a lot together shouldn't work with welding torches in their garages.

Having gathered all the materials to begin their project, they had to design a pattern for their "stained glass." Luci was making inserts for shutters that would frame her bathroom window. Alyce's inserts would be for the shutters in her kitchen.

Using their artistic natures, they were ready to make the frames. The lead was bent into shape and the liquid silver was applied at the joints. "Now," they exclaimed, "comes the easy part, baking time." They preheated the oven, put the different colors into the lead frames, set the timer, and into the oven their masterpieces went.

Usually, the aroma from their ovens is aromatic. Not so with melting plastic. Thank goodness Mother Nature cooperated and windows in the house were quickly opened. But eventually, their handiwork was complete. From a distance, their plastic creations resembled stained glass, and they were delighted.

Corn Husk Dolls and Cornucopias

After their successful "stained glass" challenge, they were on the lookout for more inspiration. They researched local craft fairs for craft ideas. On one occasion they saw homemade corn husk dolls. Quickly, they picked up the instructions accompanying the dolls and went off to buy supplies: corn husks and twine. After folding, twisting, and assembling, a doll emerged. This became a lovely fall decoration and a craft for the older girls to do at Thanksgiving.

Another fall decoration was a flour cornucopia. The beautiful centerpiece lasted throughout the season. First, they bought chicken wire and formed the cornucopia, then covered it in aluminum foil. Next they made enough dough to form long, rope-like pieces, which they twisted and turned.

Once the twisted ropes were formed, the ladies sprayed the aluminum foil with Pam, a cooking spray, and attached the coils to the form. An extra braid was added to the opening of the cornucopia, and into the oven it went. Once baked and cooled, the chicken wire frame was removed, and the dough was ready for decoration. It could hold various-shaped fruits with clusters of grapes artfully cascading from the cornucopia. Other options included using flowers or other fall decorations.

Knitting

Sometimes our crafters selected projects that they could work on both together and alone. Knitting projects fit that bill. Luci had started a sweater after her oldest son Jimmy was born that would have been perfect for the winter when he was two. However, she didn't finish it until her second son, Steve, was two. Since there is a three-year gap between them, a five-year project was not practical.

Unlike Luci's sister Lydia, a master knitter, Luci was skeptical that knitting was her "thing." But Alyce was convincing. They made several simple items like scarves and hand warmers. Alyce continues to make knitted items now for her grandchildren while Luci has made several scarves for Jim.

Sewing Underwear

In the 70s, the ladies expanded their sewing repertoire to other materials besides cotton and wool by taking the course "Sewing with Knits." Lucky for these gals, the course not only covered knits, it covered making underwear. Now that was practical.

Before long, these sewers were making underwear in all shades with matching elastic waistbands. These were not Victoria's Secret underwear, but a prettier version of Hanes cotton bloomers. Some might disparagingly call them "grannie underwear." You couldn't wear them out if you tried. Luci still has nylon and matching elastic, so there's still hope that she may one day convince Alyce to resume sewing underwear.

Window Dressing

Another sewing project involved recycling. In the 70s, drapes were popular. Luci had a beautiful set of dining room drapes made of upholstery material in a Jacobean print. Also at that time, to-the-floor dresses were popular.

After being invited to a party at one of her Mother's Club friend's houses, she decided she needed a new dress. Borrowing a page from Carol Burnett's satirical *Gone With the Wind* sketch, she "saw it in the window and she just had to have it." With all the unused extra material she had bought for those drapes, it was inevitable that the bottom of her new empire-waisted dress would be the drape material. The top would be an extra piece of blue material.

Voila! All dressed up for the party.

Holly Hobby Hats Galore

After many years of buying Sears Toughskin pants for the boys, Luci was overjoyed to make little girl dresses for Lauren-Kate. When Lauren-Kate was a toddler, Holly Hobby dolls were popular, and the ubiquitous Holly Hobby hat and prairie dress were the rage. When sewing patterns became available for both the dress and the hat, Luci became obsessed. Every trip to the Cove with Lauren-Kate produced a new hat.

"Luci, do you have an elf at home that makes them every night?" questioned Alyce when Luci arrived at the beach with Lauren-Kate sporting another new Holly Hobby hat.

"Oh, Alyce, I've got it down to a science. It takes so little fabric, and you know how much fabric I have."

"With all your fabric she'll have enough Holly Hobby hats to wear to her college graduation. She does look so cute though with her little curls peeking through the brim," admired Alyce.

"Plus, she's protected from the sun," added Luci.

Bermuda Bags

In the 70s, a wood-handled cloth bag called a Bermuda Bag was popular. Buttons on the bag's lining made the covers interchangeable. Using different materials, you could make pocketbooks to match all your outfits. Since Luci made many of her own clothes, there was plenty of extra material to fashion Bermuda bags. While initially it was fun to be coordinated, the thrill soon faded when changing covers became an integral part of leaving the house.

In cleaning her attic recently, Luci found several iterations of the bag fashioned from frocks no longer fashionable. If the fad ever comes back, she's ready.

Sewing Homemade Christmas Gifts

Through the years, these crafters often made homemade Christmas gifts. While Lauren-Kate still enjoyed dolls, Luci bought the Raggedy Ann pattern. Jill wasn't as enamored of dolls, so Alyce got a no-name doll pattern. They spent hours making the dolls, embroidering the faces, and making yarn hair and elaborate dresses. Again, it was more special to these two mothers than it was for their children, but they had many laughs.

Raggedy Ann ultimately found a home in Luci's attic. However, this loveable doll gets a different response from the grandchildren after movies like *Chuckie* and other horror films about evil dolls.

The next year, they decided to make aprons for Jill and Lauren-Kate to use as they "cooked" in their play kitchens. Again, great pains were made to produce aprons that included embroidered names and ruffled tops. And again, they ultimately were used more for decoration than their intended use. At the time, Jill and Lauren-Kate were not interested in the culinary arts that Luci and Alyce favored. They were more interested in playing with the boys in the circle. However, as they became young women, they became accomplished cooks.

Dollhouse Designers

Having struck out twice making what they thought were great gifts for Jill and Lauren-Kate, they decided to try again by making them dollhouses. What little girl wouldn't love a dollhouse? It turned into a hobby for both women.

Enrolling in a woodworking class at Whitman Hanson High School, Luci and Alyce created their own style house. Alyce had blueprints for a modest home, but Luci found the Yield House Doll House kit. A behemoth of a house, Luci's manse was a true salt box that was over three feet wide and three feet high even after she removed the back portion.

With the houses complete, they scoured every dollhouse store in the area for dollhouse wallpaper. Who knew that dollhouse wallpaper was as varied and expensive as real wallpaper? Of course, the roof had to be shingled, a very tedious task, especially with Luci's expansive roof. Stairs had to be built to reach the second floor and even Luci's attic area. They shopped for windows, doors, furniture, decorations, bedding, pots and pans—everything you would need to complete and furnish a home. Their houses had antique bathrooms with pull toilets and miniature bathroom fixtures. These houses even had electric lights.

Lauren-Kate and Jill were delighted at first, but the ardor soon waned. Now, while Alyce's house could neatly fit in a bedroom, Luci's ark couldn't. Finding the right spot proved difficult until finally it was put on the porch, where it was used more by little children who visited than it was by Lauren-Kate.

Smocking and Embroidery

Smocking and embroidery were also handcrafts Luci and Alyce enjoyed. While Luci had learned smocking from her mother, Alyce had learned from reading the pattern directions. When Alyce had her first grandchild, she smocked the christening dress. The dress has become a family heirloom used by all the baby girls with Alyce embroidering the name of each baby on the hem of the dress.

After working on time-consuming hand embroidery, they took a class in machine embroidery in June 1980 and were whipping out personalized everything on their Singer and Brother sewing machines. Every baby gift they gave had something personalized with embroidery. They learned to set the tension, make petals, French knots, appliqué, and much more. Polyester thread was never to be used because cotton thread wouldn't pucker as much.

They applied these methods to several items, but as the years progressed and their needs and time commitments changed, they found less time to pursue the hand arts.

Craft Fair

With all these projects, you would think that these gals should have gained financially but alas, their only attempt to rent a craft table at a craft fair in the Maquan School in Hanson was a disaster. It started innocently enough when they noticed that the school was holding a holiday craft fair. Since these ladies were always crafting, Alyce approached Luci one fall day. "Why don't we rent a table at the craft fair? We could make those crocheted string pocketbooks, some Christmas ornaments, and even corn husk dolls."

Alyce was so animated that Luci got sucked in immediately. "Do you think people would buy our stuff?"

"Of course they would!"

Four weeks later, their homes were strewn with a multitude of gift items. Pricing came next. Novice entrepreneurs, they priced as if they would be purchasing the items themselves. Buoyed with new energy, they eagerly packed up their treasures and headed for the fair.

"Ooh, Alyce, they gave us a table on the side next to the entrance, that's great. We have a prime spot."

Artfully displaying their wares, they eagerly awaited the first customers. Nothing sold.

"Shocked, I'm simply shocked," gasped Luci.

"Me too. Not one thing sold. Now what are we going to do with all these things?" asked Alyce.

"Your guess is as good as mine."

"House parties," Alyce shouted.

The house parties proved more successful than the craft fair. All their items sold, and they received orders for more string bags.

The Iron Comforter

One of the most memorable craft undertakings was making a queen-sized comforter for Luci's bed. After finding a fabric bargain outlet in Pawtucket, Rhode Island, Luci bought enough Martha Stewart material to completely redo the master bedroom: curtains, comforter, and bed skirt at $2.50 a yard.

Next she bought enough batting to pad the comforter. Of course, defining what is "enough" batting is relative. Luci has a reputation for supporting the philosophy that more is better. Sewing a comforter is a simple project of creating a big rectangle. But working with that much material was cumbersome, so when it came to filling the comforter, she relied on her faithful companion to help. Off to Alyce's she went.

Now a completed queen comforter measures 87″x 95″. The first step was to turn the three sewn sides right-side out to insert the stuffing in the open fourth side. With Alyce on one end and Luci on the other, they attempted the task.

"This isn't going to work Alyce."

"Okay. You go inside the comforter and grab a corner."

"If I get lost in here, call the fire department."

"I'm on it."

As Luci began her journey to the corner of the comforter, Alyce was bent over laughing. Luci's five-foot frame was engulfed in the comforter and formed a human lump across the room.

"It's not funny, Alyce. It's hot in here." Finally, Luci got to the corner and started pulling it toward the open side.

"Whew, we did it."

"Not so fast, Luci, you have to get the other side."

With steady effort and renewed zeal, she turned the comforter right side out. Now the task was to insert the filling. The batting was 1 1/2″ thick, but Luci had cut three pieces making the filling 4 1/2″ thick. No wimpy comforter was this.

Placing the batting was even more difficult. First, she had to bunch it up while trying to separate the top portion of the comforter. There wasn't much room to breathe inside the comforter, but she finally got to the corners. "Okay, Alyce, put a pin at this corner, I'm going for the next corner."

At last, the corners were in place, and she gingerly crawled out of the comforter tunnel. The process was repeated two times. Each time the space between batting and comforter cover grew smaller and Luci's moving bulge grew larger as she moved forward. What a "comforter" it turned out to be.

Alyce remarked, "You couldn't buy a comforter that thick." In fact, Jim labeled it the "iron curtain." He was afraid the weight alone would compress his breathing. But boy, it looked so thick and lush on the bed. The matching cornices on the windows completed the ensemble.

Tea Cozies

Inspiration for handcrafts sometimes came from the most unlikely sources. While having high tea at the Dunbar Tea House in Sandwich one afternoon, they commented on how cute the tea cozies were in which the little teapots were nestled. "Want to make some?" they exclaimed in unison.

That necessitated a detour after they enjoyed their high tea to The Christmas Tree Shop in Pembroke for the teapots and another stop at Joann's Fabric Store in Hanover for the fiber filler, elastic, fabric, and cord to complete the project.

Knowing that Luci never throws anything away, Alyce knew that she would have extra elastic from the double-knit jersey class. She was right. In fact, Luci didn't even buy fabric at Joann's because she had leftover material from a cotton shower curtain she had made earlier.

Without patterns and with a bit of trial and error, the cozies were made and are still used today. However, they're not used when Luci and Alyce have tea at each other's houses because one of their tea sessions lasts much too long to be satisfied by a small pot of tea.

Posh Picnic Baskets

One crisp fall day in the early 2000s, Luci said to Alyce, "The minute the weather starts to turn, I start thinking about Christmas. I've always wanted to be finished by Thanksgiving, but inevitably, I'm still running ragged on Christmas Eve."

"Do you think it's because you keep adding things to your 'to-do' list?" Alyce joked.

"It's partially your fault for finding good ideas on Pinterest."

"But Luci, we don't have to do them all," laughed Alyce.

"Seriously, we always say we're going to start earlier, but we never do, Alyce."

"Okay, then let's make those picnic baskets we saw at the shop on the Cape this summer. Now that both Karen and Pat and Jimmy and Herena are married, picnic baskets would make great gifts," mentioned Alyce.

"Oh, how romantic. Let's do it," sighed Luci.

These would be no ordinary picnic baskets. They shopped for the perfect basket and bought china plates, crystal flutes, and real silverware. Of course, such quality items wouldn't go into just any wicker basket, even if it were the ideal size and shape. These artisans lined their baskets with satin fabric to cradle the china. Elastic was sewn in to support the flutes and silverware.

Thrilled with their treasures, they assembled the baskets and were delighted with the results. In hindsight, a picnic backpack might have been more appropriate for these young moderns, but Luci and Alyce really enjoyed the creative project that nurtured their romantic spirit.

Scrapbooking

Scrapbooking was another project Alyce would procrastinate about until Luci and Alyce were invited to Blair Gill's wedding shower. At the shower, they noticed a scrapbook from Blair's mother where all the special events of Blair's life were preserved in pictures, memorabilia, and journal entries. Oh boy, Luci fell in *love* with this idea.

"Wouldn't that be a great thing for us to do for the kids?" she said.

"I don't think so. I would have to do five books," replied Alyce.

Thus it went for a few years. During those years, scrapbooking took off. Soon there were stores like Michael's that devoted whole sections to scrapbooking. Still, Alyce was reluctant. However, when Alyce's daughter Allison had a scrapbook party at her home in Plymouth, Luci and Alyce went to support her.

Now Alyce, being of a practical mind, would never normally purchase an entire collection of supplies at such a party. But purchase she did. She left the party equipped with scrapbook supplies: scissors to crop, forms to trace shapes, a paper cutter, and a beautiful case to store everything. Amazed, Luci questioned, "Who are you and what have you done with my friend?"

The scrapbooking years began. Finding the right book was important. Alyce found hers right away. "I can't wait to show you, Luci."

"Me too. I'll drop by to show you mine this afternoon after I come back from the market."

Later that afternoon with scrapbook in hand, Luci eagerly showed it to Alyce. "Do you love it?"

"Yes, very much. It's exactly what I would buy. In fact, it *is* what I bought," Alyce said as she showed Luci hers. Not surprisingly, they had bought the same book.

"Woah, that's eerie, Alyce," exclaimed Luci as they laughed over a cup of tea.

Although scrapbooking is a very enjoyable hobby, it's also an expensive one. Alyce started in reverse birth order with Jill's book. Luci also started in reverse birth order with her daughter Lauren-Kate. She wasn't sure that her boys would be as enthusiastic about a scrapbook as her daughter.

As you might guess, Alyce finished five books before Luci had finished her first one. Finally, Luci finished Lauren-Kate's book. She was so exhausted she didn't have the energy to start another one right away.

It took several years, but Luci finally finished her memory scrapbooks. Her "baby boys" were over fifty years old by then, but they seemed to relish the books more than they might have when they were young men.

CHAPTER 17

It's For the Birds

After these woodworkers had fashioned their dollhouses, their interest in woodworking only grew. With the advent of HGTV and all those home decorating shows, Luci's interest intensified. How easy the TV carpenters made miter joints look. She bought a miter saw and learned to cope, a woodworking technique of shaping the end of a molding. When she decided her fireplace looked blah, she ran wood to the ceiling and added three mitered frames and crown molding. She had a column cut in half and installed the two halves topped by crown molding to frame the inside of her front door.

Of course, none of these projects and many others went without mishap. When "ladders" were not high enough, creativity prevailed. OSHA could have initiated an investigation of unsafe working practices if they had known.

At the time, Alyce had sons-in-law that could make her designs a reality. But one day, these amateur woodworkers decided to expand their enterprising ideas to outside projects. The birdhouse building days commenced.

Both women had been using power tools now for years, but Alyce wanted to bring it up a notch. "We can use my brother's nail gun and compressor. Wait till you see how fast it is to use," Alyce raved.

"I'm used to the noise of the miter saw, but I'm kinda intimidated by how loud the compressor is."

"Yeah, but right now you have to pre-drill all the holes and then hand-nail them in. This is much faster. Let's try it on window boxes. You said you wanted two window boxes for your shed in Canada. We can each make a window box and then we can make the birdhouses." Equipped with nail gun and compressor, they set up shop in Alyce's sister Kathy's garage.

Luci arrived promptly at 10:00 sporting ear plugs, a toolbelt fastened at her waist, and eyes hidden behind large safety glasses. Popping open the car trunk, she reached in and pulled out several pieces of lumber, trying to balance the unwieldy load.

"Wow, Bob the Builder's here," Alyce remarked. "What an outfit, Luci."

"What? I can't hear you."

Alyce motioned to Luci's ears. "Take those out till we turn on the compressor."

"Oh, right. I didn't want to forget them. You know how efficient I am, Alyce," Luci laughed.

After cutting the ten pieces of wood for the window boxes, the women took turns using the nail gun. What a difference it made. Though Luci winced every time she drove a nail in, she readily admitted to Alyce that it made the job much easier. Before long, two window boxes were completed, ready to be filled with cascading flowers.

"Gee thanks, Alyce, for helping me make the window boxes."

"Now we can make the birdhouses," said Alyce.

"Let's go on Pinterest to find ideas," suggested Luci.

"Great, let's eat lunch and then look. If we find a style and it's not too late, we can go get the material today."

"Sounds like a plan," agreed Luci. She took the window boxes to her car while Alyce went in to get their salads.

But the birdhouse building would have to wait for another day because lunch and perusing Pinterest for birdhouse designs filled the rest of their afternoon.

The next week, with birdhouse designs in place, they returned to Kathy's garage. Their initial house was a very small one, but that was soon modified. In the next few days, they began working individually. Alyce's birdhouse was finished and perched in Kathy's backyard soon after. Luci needed more time because she had added a porch and other embellishments to hers.

"This would be perfect for Canada," she told Jim. To date, the fashionable birdhouse is perched in Luci's shed in Canada waiting for Jim to find the "perfect" spot for it.

The birdhouses sparked an interest. Alyce found herself making several more for family members. Luci cut out three more patterns for the small houses, and Lauren-Kate's three young boys each had a day at Luci's making and painting their very own birdhouse.

PART IV

The Financial Phase: A Gal's Got to Make a Living

CHAPTER 18

The Pastry Cart

As the late 70s approached and their children were all in school, these homemakers began to get restless. While they had plenty to do tending to their homes and families, they wanted to do more to contribute to the family coffers. They both loved to cook and were considered quite creative in their food presentations, so they thought they could combine their talents and parlay them into financial gains. Glorious plans of being entrepreneurs percolated in their brains.

"We'll be able to cook together. What fun, and we can plan parties and get paid for it," exclaimed Luci.

"And we can do it and still be home with the kids! Perfect," agreed Alyce. "This must be professional. We need business cards. We need a game plan," she added.

"My sister-in-law works for the Small Business Administration. I'll bet she'll know how we can get started. I'll call her."

That call led to a meeting at Luci's house with a representative from the Small Business Administration, a retired businessman whose job was to assist enterprising new business owners. Thus, the Pastry Cart was born.

Now, the new business owners had much to do to make this catering business a reality. First business cards were ordered, and then came the serious task of creating their menus and offerings. These potential caterers could not be faulted for a lack of energy. Perusing their recipes, they gathered their favorites. Pages and pages of menu offerings were typed.

While they didn't lack talent or enterprise, they did lack marketing skills and had a complete disregard for profit margins. For example, they offered a hundred boxed cookies for $20.00. These weren't simple cookies either. Customers could pick from the following options: mint jelly rolls, coconut jelly rolls, almond cookies, pecan sandies, fudgies, lemon slices, eclairs, or mini-Hungarian tortes. The deluxe tray for $25.00 included butterfly puff pastries, raspberry tartlets, brownies, Danish dainties, and apricot horns. They even offered cookies by the dozen for $2.00 per dozen.

Even with their limited advertising, they were overjoyed to receive their first catering job: twelve dozen cookies for $24.00. This generous offer included plating and passing the cookies around to the guests. How excited they were. They drew up the grocery list and divided the ingredients. The next day they began baking as soon as the children went to school.

The ability to work seamlessly together was remarkable. Their organizational skills could be a model for training battle troops. Ingredients were measured, KitchenAids were blaring, ovens were preheated, and finished cookies began cooling on racks on Alyce's long harvest table. Each finished cookie was garnished with icing, dusted with sugar, or topped with a pastry creme rosette.

Their attempt to complete the order before the children came home failed, and after greeting the children, giving them samples, and encouraging them to go out and play in the circle, they continued. Finally, they were finished. The cookies looked beautiful, the kitchen did not. Dirty pans and utensils surrounded them, and flour and icing spatters decorated their aprons despite their constant mantra to clean as they went. Neither could stop and enjoy their efforts until the kitchen was clean. They had time for a brief cup of tea to admire their confections before it was time to start supper.

The next afternoon, they dressed in black skirts and white blouses and brought their cookies to the party in Bridgewater. They had been so busy cooking that they hadn't settled on how much each had spent at the market. They decided that they would grab a light supper after the party and settle up then.

The hostess was very pleased. Our gals were elated as they left the party with their first paycheck. Later at the restaurant, while enjoying their salads, their joy was mitigated when they realized that their tea and salads ate up all their catering profit. Undiscouraged, they determined to try harder to increase their profit margin.

Their next catering job was a small wedding to be held at the VFW Hall in Bridgewater. The guest list included between fifty to seventy-five people. These moguls charged $8.00 per person. That included dinnerware, plastic stemware, and wine for the toast. But wait, there's more! Cake cutting and napkins were also included. But wait, there's more *again*! Set-up and cleanup of tables were also included. These perennial romantics were smitten to be part of the wedding.

Here's the menu they offered: freshly sliced roast beef, a choice of two vegetables (peas, squash, mashed potatoes with sour cream, green beans, carrots, or corn) a tossed salad, assorted relish trays, plus coffee and tea. For dessert, they offered ice cream in puff pastry with fudge sauce, or vanilla ice cream topped with chocolate sauce and fresh strawberries. Their clients didn't hesitate to accept the proposal.

Our busy cooks had to coordinate with the hall. What kitchen facilities did they have? Did they have a coffee urn? Did they have a meat slicer for the roast beef? How about utensils and spatulas? The list of questions grew. Once that information was provided, they began their preparations.

The roast beef turned out to pink perfection. You could cut it with a fork. The clients were delighted and even gave the budding entrepreneurs money beyond their contracted price. After cleaning up, our caterers realized that they had improved their profit margin at last. In fact, Luci used her $25.00 profit to buy Jim a raincoat for Christmas. Although they had doubled their profit margin, they realized they had a long way to go as business tycoons.

They decided to expand the business by going wholesale making pastries for restaurants. They made apple pie and mile-high strawberry pie to offer as samples. Their first call was to an upscale restaurant in Pembroke. After dropping off their samples, they waited anxiously at Alyce's for a call. An hour later, the phone rang. They looked at each other and yelled, "Whoopie."

"Pastry Cart," said Alyce in her most professional tone. "Uh ... sorry, no, we don't need any new magazines. No really, we know that's a good magazine, but we don't want it. Have a good day." Alyce placed the receiver back and just nodded to Luci.

"Well, it's still early Alyce. Let's have another cup of tea."

When the phone rang again, Alyce took a deep breath and answered, "Pastry Cart." Her eyes widened and she gave the thumbs up to Luci. "Well, we're glad you enjoyed the samples. Of course, we can customize any recipe. Fine. We'll pick up your recipe specifications and can get that order to you by Friday morning."

No sooner was the phone back on the wall than both these mature matrons were hugging and jumping up and down with excitement. Success at last. "They want us to bake special desserts for them. One is a Linzer Torte, another is a mocha dacquoise," gushed Alyce.

"What's a dacquoise?" Luci asked.

"I have no idea, Luci, but we have to make one by Friday. We can stop over today and get his recipes. We have to pretend we know what they are and are just looking for his specific requirements."

They discovered that the mocha dacquoise was a very rich French confection of two layers of ground hazelnuts and meringue with a butter-rich mocha and coffee liquor filling, topped with chocolate ganache. The first time they made the dacquoise, they had to pipe the meringue base with a pastry bag, which broke and managed to explode onto the ceiling. They decided to skip the piping bag for the next batch.

One week, Alyce and Luci couldn't deliver the orders and asked Jim to bring the pastries to the restaurant's delivery entrance. Not accustomed to being a delivery boy, Jim found the owner arrogant and supercilious. But he faithfully delivered the goods on time.

After they had completed the orders for about a month, they realized they had never tasted the mocha dacquoise. That was soon to change. Because the order the following week was unusually large, they brought Alyce's oldest daughter with them. As they were walking along the path to the delivery entrance, the inevitable happened.

Luci turned to see Alyce stumbling on the uneven walkway while trying unsuccessfully to balance the dacquoise. *Splat.* The dacquoise landed on the pathway.

Their motto, "When life gives you lemons, make lemonade," came in handy. They carefully scraped the dacquoise back on the plate and brought it home. Although it necessitated an extra bake and an extra trip the following day, it did give them the opportunity to taste the dacquoise. Thus, the gals introduced to their families a very delicious dessert that has become a family favorite.

At Thanksgiving, the restaurant ordered twenty-four apple pies. No way could these bakers make twenty-four pies at the last minute, so they made them ahead without baking them. They had to practically empty both their freezers to fit all twenty-four pies. On delivery day, they used both ovens to bake the pies, so the restaurant could serve genuine, homemade apple pies for the holiday.

Meanwhile, they added the dacquoise to their catering list for $15.00. The dacquoise is so rich that one dacquoise could serve at least twelve people. They discovered later that the restaurant sold a very small slice of the dacquoise and charged $4.95 for each slice. Alas, our bakers had not mastered the art of pricing.

CHAPTER 19

Career Girls in the Real World

Luci's Path

The first few years on Katydid were busy ones with Alyce and Luci adding to their houses and to their families. In 1974, Lauren-Kate Record was born. Instead of toy trucks, Luci was buying dolls and baby girl clothes. She was either tripping over Legos, feeding the baby, or being a slave to the washing machine. But by 1976, she was hungry for adult pursuits like taking a shower at times besides when all three children were sleeping. She longed for the days when she could read and discuss books. Alyce, also a reader, was very busy with her four girls, so there was no sitting on the veranda with mint juleps and a good book in their schedules.

When Luci suggested asking the new, young librarian if she could start a book club at the library, Alyce readily supported the idea. Thus, Bookbeat was born. Perhaps Luci couldn't acknowledge that although she didn't miss correcting papers, she did miss teaching high school English. This was evident in the Bookbeat format. Luci picked two books each month with other titles optional as extras. Each session had a theme, and the required books dealt with different approaches to that theme. First, she had an introductory paragraph that briefly described both books followed by detailed, thought-provoking questions or comments that would assist the group's reading and understanding of the books as well as jump-start the discussions.

Now this was overkill, but it worked because the discussions were always lively and really did explore the topics. The favorite selection the first year was *Against All Odds* by Tom Helms.

Although the book dealt with handicaps, physical and mental, its true value lay in the insights and glimpses of personal courage, fortitude, and perseverance. It was a powerful, warm, intensely moving account of Tom Helms's struggles to walk after two crippling accidents had left him a quadriplegic. His descriptions of the accident were so imagistic that the reader was riveted to the page. Yet sadness was not the pervasive mood of the book. Humor was peppered throughout, and the message was of hope and promise for the future.

Because the group enjoyed the book so much, Luci wrote the author. To her great surprise, he responded with a three-page handwritten letter. He was delighted that his book had been chosen as the favorite book of that season, and shared the status of his health and future plans. Luci has kept the letter to this day.

Somehow, for women who didn't have time to blink, they found the time to read. The meetings were held in the evening, which meant that Jim and Ron would oversee their respective crews. That was true devotion. The girls were almost giddy to find themselves talking for a whole hour without being interrupted, having to change diapers, or having their shirts tugged for attention.

Luci led the book group until 1979 when she was offered the position of Acting Librarian in Hanson. Each town was required to have a librarian that had a Masters of Library Science degree. Because Hanson did not have a librarian with that certification, the state awarded a grant that would pay the librarian to obtain her Masters in Library Science and allow the town to hire an acting librarian for that year.

Luci found the challenge exhilarating, and the year passed too quickly. The veteran staff of three was welcoming and kept the library running smoothly, giving Luci time to plan events, go through stacks of book reviews, and deal with the administrative demands of the library. But there was always time to interact with the patrons and to establish Patron's Pick, highlighted books that patrons found most enjoyable.

Both Alyce and Maggie Gill also helped during Children's Library Week by offering craft workshops. In Alyce's workshop, she taught the children to make delicate Christmas ornaments decorated with ribbon and lace. Maggie helped the children create beautiful macrame plant hangers. She also offered new plants to fit into those hangers. Both of their workshops were offered to third through fifth graders, and both workshops quickly filled up.

For sixth through eighth grade, professional dance instructor Rose Araujo taught a new line disco. A contest followed with prizes for the top dancers who were judged on the following: foot positions, rhythm, timing, originality, creativity, animation, and posture. Katydid's own Deedee Hennelly won Honorable Mention in the dance contest. She received a gift certificate for a free 45 RPM single of her choice.

A jellybean contest was held for children under twelve. Katydid had two honorable mentions: Jim Record and Steve Record.

There were activities for all holidays and school vacations. For example, during February vacation, there were Game Challenges, a movie, and Cooking Corner. The Game Challenges included checkers, where Jim Record won first place. The first-place champs received a $3.00 gift certificate to McDonald's.

Cooking Corner, which was held for grades one to six, was an overwhelming success as measured by the eager number of children who wanted seconds of Swedish meatballs, tossed green salad, homemade applesauce, and George Washington dessert crepes. Acting as chef, Luci was assisted by several friends of the library.

Authors were invited to visit regularly, and many activities for adults made for a vibrant and active year for Luci. By the end of the year, new opportunities emerged, and Luci returned to teaching.

She began what would become a twenty-six-year career with the Silver Lake Regional School District. Her first assignment was at the Silver Lake Middle School teaching English and one geography class. Then Proposition 2 1/2 passed, which forced towns to cap budgets at two and a half percent. All the gains in improving class sizes were slashed when budget cuts eliminated all new hires at the end of the school year.

Weekly trips to the unemployment office in Plymouth became "reunions" for teaching friends Luci had met that year, especially her friend Sylvana. They connected on the first day when Principal Arthur Hand introduced the new teachers. The new French and Spanish teacher Sylvana Myr was followed by Sylvana Record, the new English teacher.

Sylvana immediately looked around excited to see that someone else shared her unusual name. Luci, equally surprised at her introduction, wondered if she would be known as Sylvana all year. Instead, they discovered that although they didn't share the same first name, they had a lot in common and became very good friends.

For the last three months of that school year, Luci taught sixth grade at East Bridgewater Middle School for a teacher on maternity leave. While the children were sweet and enthusiastic, she missed discussing literature. At the end of the year, she planned to enjoy the summer and even contemplated an extended vacation in the fall.

However, that summer, Silver Lake Regional School District recalled her, this time to teach English at Silver Lake High School. The high school was a sprawling complex serving over 1,200 students from four towns: Kingston, Halifax, Plympton, and Pembroke. It was only a ten-minute commute for Luci. She loved it. Finally, she would have a captive audience to discuss books as well as writing!

Soon she would immerse herself in Silver Lake life, serving as senior class advisor and co-chair on the committee preparing for the NEASC visit to Silver Lake, as well as an evaluator on a site visit to a school in the western part of the state. Her co-chair on the preparation for the NEASC visit was Rich Kelley, who was at the time the assistant principal. While preparing the school for the evaluation was a time-consuming and challenging task, working with Rich made the job fun. In the end, Silver Lake received full accreditation from NEASC.

Luci loved teaching but still got excited when an early morning call announced, "Snow Day. No School." On one particularly memorable snow day, an unusual confluence of events occurred. The men still went to work, and both the Hennelly and Record children had school, but Silver Lake was canceled! Serendipity! Luci always knew very early when school was canceled, so she called Alyce immediately.

"Come over for breakfast, Luci," said Alyce.

"I'll be right there," Luci gushed.

Instead of the suit and high heels she had set out to wear that day, Luci donned her sweatshirt and sweatpants, popped on her snow boots, and off to Alyce's she trudged. The wind had picked up and the snow was beginning to mount. Pulling the hood up on her snow jacket, she sloshed through the mushy mix for three hundred feet to reach Alyce's door.

What a feast. Alyce had made pancakes and all the fixings. Orange juice in fluted glasses was toasted, and the next couple of hours were spent planning their next Tuesday get-together. It felt like playing hooky from school.

However, Luci's snow days became a memory and her days in the classroom were numbered. In 2002, she became a Housemaster along with Ed Dunn and Paul Viera. Rich Kelley was now principal. It was an exhilarating and challenging time. In 2004, the Town of Pembroke left the Silver Lake Regional School District and Luci was assigned to the newly formed Pembroke High School.

However, when Ed Dunn left Silver Lake to become a principal, Silver Lake recalled Luci, and she spent the rest of her career there. In addition to her other duties, she coordinated the Silver Lake School District's Mentoring Program for new teachers, a position she continued to hold for the year after she retired. Her ties to Silver Lake continued when she was called back to serve as English Coordinator for a year. It was two days a week, with no teaching assignments, just administrative duties. That sounded manageable for this retiree while leaving her time to continue meeting Alyce every Tuesday afternoon to plan activities. Retirement brought more time for family and the cottage in Canada.

Lovey's

The children were all in school now, and Luci had returned to her career in teaching. Alyce needed to return to the workforce too. She worked for several years at a lawyer's office, and then at the nuclear power plant in Plymouth. This was a fast-paced and interesting job where she helped facilitate the contractor's entry into the power plant. The plant was shut down for refueling and all the skilled construction workers needed to be badged to access the site. This included background checks of their medical and financial status, CORI checks, and anything else that might make them ineligible to access the plant.

Along with the background checks, safety classes were mandatory. Alyce worked with a team of people to make this happen. The team was under time constraints, for each man was far from home and the sooner they were badged, the sooner they started work. This resulted in sixty-hour weeks and although it was interesting work, when it ended, Alyce decided that if ever she worked that hard again, she would be working for herself.

And as life would have it, she went to a school reunion and ended up talking with a fellow classmate who told her about her business as a home daycare provider. Because Alyce's real passion was children, she was quite taken with the idea of starting her own business. Alyce decided to start a new career as a daycare provider.

Providing daycare required a state license as well as an attention to detail, excellent business acumen, an ability to multi-task, and an abundance of patience.

This time period coincided with Alyce's daughter Lauren's dilemma. She was struggling with having to go back to work and wanted to stay at home with her son Michael. The solution was obvious; they would start up a daycare business together.

They contacted the Department of Children's Services and asked about the specifics of opening an in-home daycare. The process was daunting. They had to create a business plan, be trained in CPR, take the appropriate classes required by the state, draft a contract, and decide on a location. After completing these requirements, they began to create the daycare environment in Alyce's basement.

Because half the basement was already a play area for her children, Alyce and Lauren began cleaning the space, painting the walls, gathering the toys, acquiring the bedding, and purchasing school, art, and crafts supplies. While they created a warm and inviting learning space, they also had to childproof the house upstairs where the children entered. For example, they covered all the electrical outlets and installed child-proof locks on the kitchen cabinets.

They were now ready to pursue their chosen career. They needed a name for their new business and chose Lovey's, an endearing name Alyce's dad called his children and grandchildren. They advertised in the local paper and waited.

Their first clients were children of friends. Then one day a woman came to the house looking for someone to take care of her two-year-old. Now it was official: their first real client was under contract. They were so excited; this was really going to happen. Their clientele grew and so did their business.

Alyce joined a local club of women who also were daycare providers. This turned out to be extremely valuable. She networked with these ladies each week discussing curricula, discipline techniques, and even shared referral lists.

The daycare business can be incredibly rewarding. The joy they found came from the children themselves. Lauren and Alyce didn't just want to care for the children, they wanted to prepare them for school. Embracing that philosophy, they prepared a weekly schedule that included lesson plans in science, math, reading, and music. For example, "Dancing Raisins" taught the children about chemical reactions. The walls were covered with different kinds of shapes, one of which made Alyce ask Lauren "What is that?" Turns out it was a trapezoid. You're never too old to learn something new. The bookshelves were filled with books from *Goodnight Moon* to Dr. Seuss classics.

These little ones were like sponges. They absorbed everything that was presented to them and when it was time for them to go to kindergarten, they were able to read.

With the success of the daycare, more space was needed, and thus Lovey's Too was created in Lauren's home. They could then accommodate all their clients.

In 2001, after six years of providing daycare to more than twenty-five children, Alyce retired. This was bittersweet, for she loved those little ones and now had to let them go.

Lauren has been the director of Lovey's Too for twenty-six years and the legacy continues. In 2020, Alyce's granddaughter Tyla became the director of Lovey's and Beyond.

CHAPTER 20

High Rollers and Low Expectations

Neither Alyce nor Luci were Minnesota Fats. Luci's only gambling experience was the high-stakes experience of a bingo game. Alyce, however, had a genetic advantage as her mother and sisters were both avid fans of the casinos and took excursions to them frequently. Ron and Alyce had gone to Mohegan Sun, a casino in Uncasville, Connecticut, owned by the Mohegan Tribe. On one occasion, Ron hit the jackpot and won $2,400.00! In those days, that was a considerable amount.

Giddy with delight and eager to share her good fortune, Alyce told Luci a trip to Foxwoods, a casino owned by the Mashantucket Pequot Tribal Nation in Ledyard, Connecticut, was inevitable. Foxwoods was about two hours away, so they left after the commuter traffic with enough time designated for enjoying the casino, having lunch, and getting home before dark.

The casino was a sprawling behemoth with over two hundred and fifty gaming tables and many restaurants. The decorating theme was an Indian motif with an indoor waterfall. The lighting was dim, with most of the light coming from the colorful gaming machines that noisily announced winners. The air was smoky, and many of the patrons puffed away as they pulled the arms of the slot machines. The sound of quarters cascading from the slots encouraged the gamblers that they too could win big.

Since Luci had a hard time shuffling a deck, she eschewed the more complicated games for the slot machines. Alyce only did the slots too. It didn't take long for the blinking lights and the ka-ching of the machines to get the adrenaline going.

Alas, Luci didn't have the same experience as Ron. It didn't take long for Luci to lose the entire $70.00 that she had brought. Alyce lost about $80.00. Unlike the odds at the gaming tables, the odds that one could score an inexpensive meal were good. Food was readily available and affordable. Obviously, keeping the customers fed was a priority to keeping them at the casino. Unfortunately, our gamblers weren't there long enough to get hungry for lunch.

"Well, Alyce, how are we going to explain that we lost money and had a good time?"

"It was disappointing, but we set limits, we tried, and now we know that this will never happen again."

"Well, we can recoup this with a good lunch at a restaurant with a water view."

"You had me at lunch."

PART V

The Celebration Phase: Girls Just Want to Have Fun

CHAPTER 21

Ghosts and Goblins on Katydid

Headlines warning parents of tainted candy, razors in apples, and other worrisome problems plagued the Halloween trick-or-treat ritual. Katydid mothers decided that it was safer to have home parties. Alternating houses each year, they tried to spook the children with cold green grapes in a bowl. They would blindfold the kids and have them feel around the bowl while suggesting the bowl contained eyeballs.

The children also bobbed for apples, but these were no ordinary apples. Our gals put coins in them. Cautious about choking hazards, these mothers left the coins visible near the stem of the apple. Bobbing for apples took on new meaning as the children eagerly ate their apples after bobbing.

Candy was always a great motivator. One year at Alyce's Halloween party, as three-year-old Steve was helping himself to an unguarded bag of candy, Alyce captured the startled but sheepish look on his face with a Polaroid.

Another activity that Jill remembers fondly was the Hanging Donut Challenge. Children tried to be the first to finish eating a sugar donut hanging from a string with their hands tied behind their backs.

Bobbing back and forth trying to bite the donuts left them with powder-sugared, Casper-like faces as they struggled to win the challenge.

One year at Luci's, Steve, Jimmy, and Lauren-Kate created a haunted house in their cellar. Since Luci has always been a saver, the cellar was scary in its natural state. They added fake cobwebs, though nature had enhanced their efforts with the real thing.

Background cackling and other eerie sounds emanated throughout the room. They had a bowl of wet spaghetti labeled "intestines." A rocking chair on a string was moving as if by itself. Hidden by sheets, Steve or Jimmy would stick their hands in a bucket of ice water, reach out, and grab the unsuspecting guests as they walked by.

Homemade costumes were the order of the day for the children and were often passed down from one child to the next. Alyce and Luci made clown costumes, princess costumes, Batman and Robin costumes, and 50s-era costumes. Luci's Lauren-Kate once went as Wonder Woman to align with her brothers as Batman and Robin. Allison wanted to be an angel and was so happy to see her angel wings drying in the cellar—a sure sign the rest of the costume was soon to come.

As the children got older, they became more creative. For example, one year Steve created a Hulk costume. His young frame was suddenly muscular with an oversized sweatshirt filled with batting. His pillow-inflated chest completed the transformation. The finishing touch was the green makeup that covered his face and hands. He posed for the requisite Halloween picture in Hulk-like fashion.

The real test came the next morning when it took Hulk-like scrubbing to remove the green paint. In fact, he had to explain why he looked so peaked the next morning in school.

Alyce and Luci couldn't let a holiday pass without special food. Besides the eyeball grapes and caramel apples, there were other homemade treats like popcorn balls, pumpkin cookies, and soup in a pumpkin tureen.

Adults also got into the Halloween act when, one year, the Gills hosted an adult party. Jim was a pirate, Luci a harem dancer, Ron a witch, and Alyce a dwarf. Other costumes were Darth Vader, Yoda, and gypsies. That year Ron, a sprinkler superintendent, was called back into work in the middle of the party. He had to work all night. Not his favorite Halloween.

CHAPTER 22

Progressive Dinners

In the 80s, progressive dinners were the rage, and Luci and Alyce wanted to take advantage of this new trend with their neighbors the Gills, and their friends the Edwards. Each couple would choose a particular part of the meal.

Because every couple lived on Katydid except Roger and Angela Edwards, the Edwards chose to serve the hors d'oeuvres. Angela's Italian culinary skills shone in the beautiful antipasto platter and cheese tray. Had they stayed longer, there would have been no appetite left to whet.

Alyce and Ron left a few minutes before the rest of the couples because they had the soup course. Alyce put a lot of thought into the presentation. The right china, silverware, napkins, tablecloths, stemware for the wine, flowers, and name cards merited consideration. With everything arranged, the big moment arrived, and the guests were on their way.

As the group entered Alyce's house, the aroma of creamed broccoli soup filled the air. The table was beautifully set, and the rich green soup decorated with a swirl of cream complemented the china. Pulling Alyce aside, Luci excitedly asked, "What a beautiful set of china, Alyce. I didn't even know that you *had* china."

Rolling her eyes, Alyce replied, "I didn't."

The night was going quite well when Ron, who always liked to insert humor, revealed to their friends that the progressive dinner had cost him a pretty penny. Reluctantly, Alyce explained to the group how this beautiful china service came about.

"When I picked the soup, I realized I didn't have anything nice to put the soup in. The children's cereal bowls wouldn't do. I needed some proper china. Off to the store I went in search of the nicest china set I could afford. At Rich's Department store in Plymouth, I was thrilled to find a lovely pattern with light green and gold trim." Turning to Ron with a big smile, she announced, "Ron is now the proud owner of a lovely china set that he never thought he would need."

"It'll last a lifetime and it looked beautiful," Luci added, "but time to move on to the Gills."

Across the street they went to savor a delicious roast beef main course. Thankfully, the dinner was hours long, so there was time to digest each course. The men were in their glory with the beef. Although the ladies were full after the first course, they managed to sample everything.

The group finally waddled to Luci's for dessert and coffee. One of the most popular desserts at the time was cheesecake, so that's what Luci made. Hardly a light offering, the cheesecake was a favorite among the men. Diet-conscious women relied on the coffee to complete the evening. Luci had set up a coffee and tea station so that coffee or tea could be embellished with Bailey's Irish cream, Grand Mariner, freshly whipped cream, or fresh lemon for tea. The evening continued with more conversation and laughter, making for a thoroughly enjoyable evening with good friends.

CHAPTER 23

Office Christmas Parties

Whether these ladies worked in an office or not was irrelevant. They liked the concept. One December morning after the children had gone to school, Luci called Alyce, "Alyce, Jim won the raffle yesterday at his Christmas party, a beautiful basket of chocolate and fruit. Take a break and come over and I'll make tea to go with the chocolate."

"Okay, yummy. I can't pass up chocolate," said Alyce. "I'll be right there."

Within minutes, they were munching on chocolates and sipping tea.

"Luci, why can't we have an office Christmas party? We're always working on projects, so let's go out and enjoy a holiday party," argued Alyce.

"Yeah, we create the holiday houses. Now it's time for us to get the holiday spirit," Luci exclaimed as they raised their teacups and toasted, "Here's to the first annual office Christmas party."

The ladies would forgo their customary casual attire and dress up in their holiday best. This was not a time to skimp, so they would select an upscale restaurant to celebrate. Their purpose was not solely to taste gourmet food. They were there to scout out the holiday decor, notice the presentation of the food, and critique the restaurant for inspiration. In essence, it was a working assignment.

What ideas could they incorporate into their own homes? No detail was to be missed. Trees, garlands, lighting, table settings, color combination? Was there a theme? Gingerbread men, angels, dazzling ornaments?

The only variable was the weather. Neither Alyce nor Luci was fond of driving in inclement weather. One December evening, the weather did not cooperate with their plans to go to Boston. They decided to go to a restaurant in Hanson. Off to Cataldi's they went. The restaurant was not crowded, and they could sit wherever they liked. They chose the diamond-paned bay window overlooking the landscaped area. The landscape up-lighting was ablaze, and rays of light streamed through the pine trees.

Normally the beverage of choice was tea, but this view called for a glass of wine. While they sipped their wine, snow started to fall, and the night turned magical. Somehow they giggled throughout this magical evening. A more cynical observer might have thought that perhaps the wine enhanced their interpretation of the scene. They acknowledged that the only thing that would have made it even better would have been if Jim and Ron were with them.

However, their keen eyes didn't miss the impact of landscape backyard lighting. That office Christmas party led to expanded lighting displays in their backyards. Luci lit her "Charlie Brown" tree and decorated her picnic table with lanterns. Alyce put a flower box out front with tea lights and greenery. Inspiration found. Mission accomplished.

Another memorable Christmas office party venue was the Boston Harbor Hotel. This time the weather cooperated and it was a lovely December afternoon. The dining room was quite elegant, and for this occasion, it was enhanced with holiday decor. The waiter brought them to a linen-topped table strewn with rose petals. The crystal flutes glistened, and each china setting was topped with a gingerbread man wrapped in cellophane and secured with a red ribbon. The holiday mood was set. Only a Scrooge could have resisted capturing the spirit of the season. The lunch was equally delicious, and as they left with their gingerbread men, they shared ideas on incorporating the theme in their homes.

That year Luci's kitchen was festooned with gingerbread men hanging from the panes of her angle bay window and a large gingerbread house on her counter. The aroma evoked Christmas throughout the house. She even made gingerbread ice cream sandwiches as favors for the children at her annual extended-family Christmas party.

Alyce also used the gingerbread theme in her home. After making her gingerbread men, she put a grandchild's name on each one and hung them from her kitchen garland.

On another December, the office party was at the Ritz in Boston. Although seeing the lights in Boston would have been especially memorable, these Hansonites weren't as adventurous as to take the train into the big city at night. They chose an afternoon trip instead. Having had an incredible high tea experience at the Ritz that summer, they were primed to be inspired.

However, the Ritz was under new management. The dining room was lovely but not exceptionally so. They were seated at a small table in the center of the dining area, not the most desirable location. Since they could have a good time in a bunker during a tornado, they were optimistic the Ritz would live up to its reputation. However, they were disappointed that their memories of the "Old Ritz" were not duplicated.

Solstice in Kingston proved a much better experience. Its proximity to Hanson made it a candidate for an evening dining delight. Since our ladies are not night owls, their 5:00 p.m. reservation was perfect. Their ten-minute ride brought them past houses and trees adorned with colorful lights ablaze.

Since this was a weekday, no other holiday party was scheduled at the restaurant. They were led past the bar area to a smaller, more intimate stepped-down area with a huge brick fireplace and only about six linen-topped tables, creating a private dinner party atmosphere. The food was delicious, and the atmosphere was enchanting. Although they didn't find specific decor inspiration, they reinforced their enjoyment of the holiday season. Of course, they also laughed a lot.

Patrizia's in Plymouth was selected for one office Christmas party because Luci had found an advertisement that Patrizia's had a special dinner for two for $49.00 on Wednesdays. This included a bottle of wine, a three-course meal, and dessert! Irresistible! The restaurant opened at 4:00 p.m., so that's when they arrived. Again, they had the entire dining room to themselves. They sat near the fireplace, which they both noticed was uniquely covered in stacked stone. Very modern. A quick picture was taken for future reference. Their daughters were modern in their decor, so the ladies were always on the lookout for new ideas.

The waiter poured them wine and the evening began. The restaurant offered three choices for the main course, one of which was haddock. Since these diners order fish 99 percent of the time, the haddock was a perfect choice.

Then came dessert. These gals usually don't order dessert. Alyce is always too full and often only finishes half her meal. Luci consistently finishes her meal but was also full this time. However, being full never stopped Luci from indulging in dessert, especially when the offering was crème brulée. What a treat. Even Alyce partook.

The coffee was delicious. Since they only had one glass of wine each, there was wine left over, which the waiter said they could take home! They were definitely in the holiday spirit after this office party.

The following year Trattoria, a small Italian restaurant with warm, inviting decor in Hingham, was the venue. Their waiter guided them through their choices and was very entertaining. After they had a delicious and filling meal, the waiter brought over a dessert cart of everything from chocolate mousse to cheesecake to many artfully decorated desserts. Although Luci was tempted, Alyce remained the sane one and they were able to resist. Luci had to be satisfied with the rich Italian coffee.

The Scarlet Oak Tavern was the site of one of our favorite office parties. While there is a tavern-like atmosphere in the front section with lots of dark wood, rustic beams, and colonial touches, the elegant main dining area far from the bar fit the criteria for a holiday party. Entering, they were cradled in warmth from the flickering fireplace. On the linen-covered tables, lighted hurricane lamps cast a soft glow. Because the memories of the cold, slushy outdoors hadn't left them completely, they were intrigued when their waiter recommended a warm hot toddy to begin the evening. A reasonable choice.

It's amazing how rum can change an ordinary cup of tea. How they managed to create a drink that didn't taste as if it had alcohol in it was remarkable.

Everything that followed was flavorful. They chose salmon with Romesco sauce. It was so delicious that they vowed to make Romesco sauce at home. After coffee and reminiscing on the year's activities and upcoming goals for the coming year, they left after another successful office Christmas party.

CHAPTER 24

Happy Holidays

Holidays were always a very special time for the ladies to enjoy old family traditions and create new ones of their own. Christmas time at Alyce's childhood home was enchanting. On Christmas morning, the Warner children would awake to a living room that had been transformed into a Jordan Marsh holiday window display. Presents were arranged artfully around the room: a new bathrobe draped over an armchair, dolls tucked into a baby carriage, new roller skates with a shiny new skate key under the tree, a fluffy powder puff sitting atop a round box of dusting powder, a cowgirl outfit complete with hat, pistol, and holster, and a chemistry set propped against a Lincoln Log set.

One year after all the presents were found, Alyce's mom and dad brought Alyce's brothers, Tom and Michael, to the basement where an elaborate race car set was atop the ping pong table. Sharing the joy and excitement with her siblings and seeing the happiness on her mother's face and the twinkle in her dad's eyes, Alyce felt the spirit of Christmas.

Alyce's children wanted their presents wrapped in shiny paper and ribbons to make the morning last a little longer. She acquiesced and most of the presents got wrapped, but Alyce couldn't resist the temptation to display some of the toys as her mother had. Christmas Eve, Lauren read the poem, "A Visit from St. Nicholas" to the younger girls, and stockings were hung. Christmas Mass in the morning, or midnight Mass when the girls got older, was the norm.

Traveling to the grandmothers' houses for dinner, alternating years between Nana Hennelly and Nana Warner on Christmas Day, seemed to work well until the girls wanted to stay home and play with their new toys. At that time, relatives started to come to Alyce's house for Christmas Eve gatherings or Christmas Day dinner. The day after Christmas was always a treat. They all stayed in their pj's that day and played with all the games Santa had brought.

When Luci was a child, Christmas was *the family holiday*! First, there had to be a real tree, and a big one, majestically placed in the "parlor." That was the room that was always figuratively cordoned off like a museum piece by the French doors. The room made a grand entrance on special occasions or during hurricanes, when Luci's mom would move the sofa and the three sisters, Luci, Lydia, and Linda would sit on the sofa and watch the many hurricanes of Luci's childhood. But at Christmas time, the "parlor" was all decked out in Christmas finery.

Right after Thanksgiving, Luci's dad would bring the huge Lucky Strike box filled with ornaments up from the cellar, and the decorating would begin. He was meticulous and would neatly and evenly place the colored lights on the tree. Then the girls would put the myriad of old-fashioned ornaments randomly on the tree. The piece de resistance was the tinsel. On this addition, there would be no dispute. No throwing it on the tree, no haphazard placement. For Luci's dad, this was a labor of love, as he carefully placed each piece of tinsel on the tree. For the girls, it seemed to take forever.

Luci's mom was busy in the kitchen making her fruitcake, which was to be basted over the next three weeks with alcohol. She brought out cocoa topped with marshmallow fluff and her Christmas cookies. Because there had always been homemade desserts after every meal at Lucinda Lagarto's house, Luci was always surprised to discover that some families didn't always have dessert, or that they considered fresh fruit a dessert. A shocking revelation!

At last, the house lights were dimmed and the tree was lit. Spectacular. The tinsel covered the entire tree and its gossamer shimmer was magical.

Christmas Eve in the Lagarto family meant visiting the extended family. As guests entered, a chorus of voices would sing Portuguese holiday songs. Tables of food, including filhoses and bola, were the focus. There is no such thing as a small Portuguese meal. Luci's favorite was her Aunt Mary's Portuguese crème brulée and bisquoits, recipes that Aunt Mary guarded jealously.

Luci's grandmother, called Little Vozina, always slept over Christmas Eve. The three granddaughters adored her, and each wanted her to sleep next to them. In the morning, Luci's grandfather would arrive early. Mornings became a crazy mix of three young girls practically tripping over each other to see the tree strewn with wrapped presents.

While the adults grabbed coffee and bola, the girls were too excited to eat. Luci's mother would distribute the presents from Santa, and each girl opened one present at the same time. There was always an equal number of presents, including three identical homemade pajamas. The last present would be from the grandparents, and it was always what the girls had placed at the top of their Santa lists.

Many of Luci's childhood traditions continued in the Record household. Christmas Eve always included food and the opening of one present. As they got older and bought each other gifts, the children would open these presents and one from Mom and Dad. Stockings were also hung. Luci had made four monogrammed stockings, but Father Jim insisted that his very large, red, faded, and well-worn childhood stocking would complement the four calico stockings. Homemade eggnog and Christmas cookies followed.

That night, Jimmy, Steve, and Lauren-Kate would all sleep in one room. The rule was that the next morning, they had to wait on the landing until given the signal by Luci, who was filming the production. Then, with a tumultuous roar, they would bounce down the stairs to tear into their overflowing stockings and attack the stack of wrapped presents as Luci tried to replicate her mom's "one person at a time" rule.

After a big breakfast, the children had an afternoon of playing with presents in pj's before leaving in the evening for Rhode Island to share the holiday with the extended family. The presents kept them occupied, so they never went out to play with friends that day. These scenes were likely replicated in many homes in those years, except for one fact. Although the children thought it was Christmas Day, it was really Christmas Eve. The reason Luci kept this ruse up was that she was determined that the Record Christmas would be special and not something that was done *after* the extended family Christmas party. Yet she didn't want her parents to miss out on sharing the day.

It was easy to keep this deception from the children in the early years because when they left for Rhode Island on Christmas Eve, only Christmas carols played on the radio after 6:00 p.m. Their first stop was her aunt's in Cumberland, and then to Bristol where her sisters, their families, and her mom and dad were. The food and festivities continued as everyone slept over.

Because Alyce and Luci had such wonderful memories of childhood Christmases, they began in October to make lists of all the supplies they would need to make one homemade gift each year. A bathrobe, a dollhouse, a picnic basket, an apron, a homemade doll, or even doll clothes were made. They would meet at one another's houses to sew and assemble their homemade projects.

Next was Christmas cookie and candy making. Thousands of cookies have been made over the years, and each family had their favorites. Apricot horns and raspberry Ischl tartlets were two recipes that had to be made for the holiday.

One year Luci bought alcohol for macerating fruit for her Italian-style, fruit-filled cookies. However, with so many cookies being made that year, she forgot about that batch of macerating fruit tucked in the back of the refrigerator, and that fruit continued to swim in its alcoholic bath for an entire year. However, the next year, those well-macerated, fruit-filled Italian cookies were a hit, with many people raving about the flavor.

These cooks work so well together that they have perfected the assembly-line approach, and an incredible number of delicacies were made in each get-together with laughter and tea flowing.

Decorating the house was always a treat. Pre-Pinterest, they would scan all the latest Christmas magazines to decide on new ideas for the holidays. They both liked the scent of a live tree, for it brought back memories of childhood Christmases. Luci's husband Jim, loving that a balled Christmas tree could be planted after the holiday and enjoyed in the landscaping for many years, would purchase their tree at Wyman's Garden Center. Anxious to start decorating, Luci couldn't wait until the weekend for Jim to bring the tree in. She forgot, however, that balled trees are very heavy. One year, transporting the tree from the yard to the house became a problem. Alyce to the rescue. They dragged, then rolled, then pushed the tree up the front stairs until they were exhausted. Thankfully, down the street drove Alyce's daughter Lauren, who saw the ladies in distress and immediately stopped to help.

"Oh, Lauren, you have your good coat on," sighed Luci.

That didn't stop Lauren. Grabbing the root ball with both hands, she picked that tree up and four steps later, it was in the house. Problem solved. She became Wonder Woman to our damsels in distress.

In the nineties, they began to include the making of gingerbread houses. The houses had mansard roofs, gable roofs, melted sugar panes for the windows, square pretzels for windowpanes, and were decorated with all kinds of candies. Along with the construction of these sweet confections came many a burnt finger trying to glue the pieces of the houses together with melted sugar. Pieces frequently collapsed until they discovered meringue powder, which became the magic glue to frame their houses.

On one of their thrifting days in Rhode Island, Alyce found a mold you could use to make a small gingerbread house. They were excited to use that for a while. Luci thought that with everything else they had to do at Christmas, a permanent solution was necessary. She cut a pattern out of 1/4" plywood, constructed her house, and decorated it with royal icing and candies. That served for several years, but then Luci became nostalgic for the "real" thing, and she went back to making smaller gingerbread houses. Alyce made hers from scratch; it is a tradition she has continued with her grandchildren. She would make houses for all the grandchildren, buy all sorts of candies, and then have a decorating party. Each grandchild would leave with his/her own decorated confection.

Although Ron and Alyce eventually became snowbirds, they always returned to Massachusetts for the holidays. Decorating for the holidays was still of great interest to Alyce, so over to Luci's Alyce went to help *her* decorate trees and hang outside lighting and garlands. "How grand it was working together," thought Alyce.

Having Alyce's help was a godsend for Luci. Not only was the job done in half the time, but it was always twice the fun.

On other holidays, the children woke to little gifts to celebrate the occasion. St. Patrick's Day was celebrated at Alyce's house with green mashed potatoes and lots of songs sung by the Irish Rovers. Wearing something green to school was a must for both households. Luci's mother-in-law was thoroughly Irish, with a maiden name of Malarkey. Yet Jim wasn't a fan of corned beef and cabbage, so Luci would make Irish soda bread. Before Luci's mom knew Jim's mom's maiden name, she would always say, "You're full of malarkey." Jim was too polite to comment, but he wanted to add, "Just half full of Malarkey."

Valentine's Day always involved a special breakfast table with red napkins and tiny gifts on each place setting. Chocolate was also an absolutely necessary component.

One year the ladies made giant chocolate kisses. A plastic funnel was used for a mold. First, they placed aluminum foil over the small hole in the funnel. Next, melted chocolate wafers were poured into the funnel. The funnel was placed on a glass for balance and the chocolate was allowed to cool in the refrigerator. After the chocolate was cooled and solid, the aluminum foil stopper was removed, and the chocolate was separated from the funnel and wrapped in aluminum foil. Putting a strip of paper with the child's name or a special message on the top of the giant kiss completed the project.

Sometimes it was chocolate heart-shaped lollipops, other times it was heart-shaped cookies. Anything to remind their families how much they loved them. Food was often their love language.

Easter comes after a long, cold winter, and it was quite delightful to work with pastel colors. Crochet thread came into play once when they wanted to make Easter eggs. They blew up a balloon to the size of the egg they wanted. Crochet thread was soaked in liquid starch and then wrapped around the balloon, leaving an opening in the front of the egg. Once the thread dried, they popped and removed the balloon. They added Easter grass and jellybeans to complete the decoration.

They made sweet bread chicks and bunnies, a favorite of the children and so yummy. Luci also made molded sugar eggs that were then decorated with royal icing. Little scenes were placed inside. To this day she uses these eggs at Easter time, especially when she hosts her annual extended family Easter dinner, which always includes an egg hunt.

For the egg hunt, plastic eggs are strewn in the backyard, some filled with coins, some with jellybeans, and some with real paper currency. One year, though, a couple of the paper money eggs weren't found and neither Luci nor Jim could remember where they were hidden. After that, Luci wrote the money amount on slips of paper and only distributed the real money to the winners at the end of the hunt.

PART VI

The Traveling Phase: Cars, Trains, and Planes

CHAPTER 25

High Teas

A favorite dining choice for Alyce and Luci was high tea. For those unfamiliar with this British-inspired ritual, a little background is required. In 1662, the exiled Charles II and his Portuguese bride, Catherine de Braganza, both confirmed tea drinkers, returned to the English monarchy. He brought the foreign delicacy to England, and Catherine's influence made tea popular among the wealthier classes.

Afternoon high tea was introduced in England by the Duchess of Bedford, Anna Russell, in 1840. Dinner in her household was served fashionably late at eight in the evening, and Anna found it much too long to go from breakfast to dinner without some sustenance. The duchess asked that a tray of tea, cakes, bread, and butter be brought to her bedroom late in the afternoon. This became a habit of hers, and soon she would invite her friends to join her in the dining room for afternoon tea.

Modern high tea involves tea, of course, but it is also accompanied by a tiered tray that includes the following: warm scones and assorted tea breads like date, cranberry, or banana. This is served alongside clotted or Devonshire cream and assorted jams. The second tier contains tea sandwiches. These dainty sandwiches change according to the establishment. On the top tier is an assortment of miniature desserts. Each person has her own pot of tea and tiered tray or a large tray with doubles of each selection that serves two people.

Luci was especially obsessed with finding places that served high tea and even researched places when she and Jim went on vacation. She's had high tea in Hawaii, Canada, Florida, and many other locations. At first, Jim was reluctant to believe that dainty "girly" food would fill him. He has since come to enjoy high tea almost as much as Luci.

There was no need to convince Alyce. She loved it too. High tea was something Alyce wanted to share with Ron, but it never appealed to him. However, on a Holland American cruise to the Baltic and Russia, Alyce seized the moment. Teatime was scheduled every day at three in the afternoon in the main dining room.

Ron's biggest objection to tea was that he wouldn't have enough to eat. Those little tea sandwiches and pastries didn't look as if they would satisfy a hungry man. But to please Alyce, they dressed for tea and sat at a table with a water view. When Alyce thinks of that day, she remembers Ron sipping tea holding his teacup with his pinky in the air, enjoying his crumpets.

One of Luci and Alyce's favorite spots was the Dunbar Tea Room in Sandwich, Massachusetts. Although the menu included a myriad of teas, Alyce always ordered blackcurrant and Luci always ordered apricot tea. In most restaurants, the tea sandwiches are crustless canapé-like sandwiches. However, at the Dunbar, one of the sandwiches was a curried chicken salad served on a French baguette. Cucumber sandwiches and salmon sandwiches, along with the tea breads and desserts that always included something chocolate, completed the menu.

While they always finished their individual teapots, the ladies never finished their food. There was always something to take home to Jim and Ron. Alyce was also impressed with the number of windows along the back wall that showcased the landscaping and gardens. Since her sister Kathy was adding an addition, Alyce was eager to share this design with her. Our gals are observant and always on the lookout for new design ideas.

The Ritz was at the top of their list for high teas. However, getting to it wasn't without challenges. Their first difficulty was trying to maneuver the complex parking payment system in Hanson. They were sure that Luci's car would be ticketed when they returned. They vowed to have one of the husbands drop them off next time instead of trying to figure out the new system.

In the nick of time, their train arrived, and they scurried on board, quickly found their seats, and started chatting away. Sometimes it's perplexing how they see each other so often but never run out of things to say. Unfortunately for them, they were soon approached by the conductor who informed them they were seated in the "silent car." Out of all the cars on the train, they had selected the "no talking" one. With new seats and a chastened attitude, they continued the ride to South Station.

"We're here," Alyce said. "We can walk to the Ritz. It isn't far."

"Er ... my feet will be the judge of that, Alyce. These heels are strictly for show."

Unfortunately, Alyce's definition of "not far" and Luci's were vastly different. Luci felt like the little kid on a road trip who kept asking, "Are we there yet?" Finally, several blisters later, they arrived at the Ritz.

It was all worth it! They entered the elegantly appointed dining room with music from a harp wafting through the air. They were escorted to big, comfy, high-back chairs. The room was mostly filled with women. In one corner was what appeared to be a grandmother with her two granddaughters dressed in white sundresses. In another corner were two elderly "grande dames" sipping their tea. It was a people watcher's delight.

Their observations stopped when the food was served. Everything was delicious. The jams were served in tiny individual containers, so they made a point of not using one so they could take it home. The teapots were silver and the china was monogrammed. The music played throughout the tea. It was so relaxing and delightful. Released from the constraints of her high heels, Luci's feet enjoyed a brief respite hidden under the tablecloth that draped to the floor.

The relaxation ended when they realized they had to catch the 4:30 p.m. train back. The walk back was more of a trot, but they made it. The train was packed with commuters, but they managed to find seats together so they could regale themselves with the wonderful time they had had. Thankfully Luci's car was still there when they got back, un-ticketed.

Now cautious about train parking, these high tea seekers had Jim drop them off at the train station next time to avoid parking fee hassles. Their destination was the Four Seasons in Boston. They arrived early and decided to do a bit of shopping at Macy's. On this day, Macy's was having free makeup application demonstrations. As they passed the counter, the makeup artist asked, "Would either of you gals want your makeup done?" She must have recognized Luci's minimalistic style of a dab of blush and lipstick because she looked right at her. Here was virgin territory ripe for improvement.

Always a good sport, Alyce said, "We're early, go ahead and do it."

Climbing up on the chair, Luci prepared herself for her makeover. From her magical makeup box, the artist prepared the canvas. One cream followed another. Luci was patted, creamed, and sprayed. Then her eyes were transformed with shadow, eyeliner, and mascara. Her lips were outlined and then filled in with the newest shade of lipstick. Half an hour later, the canvas was revealed. The mirror revealed a decidedly improved Luci, but she still wasn't a convert to makeup magic. "What a lot of work to look natural."

Knowing that with her lack of skill she could never reproduce those results, Luci bought the lipstick, the only product she knew how to use correctly. As she blinked through mascara-heavy eyes, she was ready for the Four Seasons.

The Four Seasons high tea was decidedly different from other high teas. First, it wasn't in the dining room. The tiered trays were brought into one of the lounge areas. The tea drinkers sat on sofas and high-back chairs. While the setting was elegant, it didn't have that feeling that usually accompanied their high tea experience. It felt less intimate, and because it was in an open area, it didn't convey the ease of lingering teatime. However, the food was among the best they had had, and as always, the company made it a wonderful experience. Of course, running to the station in heels to make their 4:30 p.m. departure was not fun.

Meanwhile, their reliable husbands waited at the train station. When the train stopped at Hanson, many harried commuters and exhausted shoppers quickly exited, but not *their* shoppers. As the train pulled out of the station, Ron and Jim noticed their wives still on the train chatting away. "I can't believe they missed their station," exclaimed Jim.

"Well, the only thing we can do is go home and wait to hear from them, but Alyce doesn't have a phone."

"Luci has one. Hopefully, she has it charged, and they don't end up in Plymouth."

Happily chatting away on the train, the ladies were oblivious to their faux pas. Suddenly the conductor announced, "Next stop, Halifax." They stared wide-eyed at each other as they realized the previous stop should have been their stop. Normal people might panic at the thought that they were now stranded. These two just burst into nervous laughter.

"We have to get off here and call them. We'll probably be in Halifax before they can get home," said Alyce.

"I hope they go home directly or we're in big trouble, Alyce."

By the time they arrived at Halifax, it was dark. After a few riders quickly headed to their cars, Alyce and Luci were alone. Unlike the Hanson station, which is nestled in a brightly lit center of commercial enterprise, Halifax is in a remote area with no other observable establishments within view. The scene looked perfect for a Lifetime movie fraught with terror.

Once the train left the station, the dense forest of pines and maples took on a menacing appearance shadowed in the lights that lined the track. However, the road leading from the platform to Holmes Street, Route 36 was so distant that it was nearly indiscernible.

"OMG Alyce, it's so dark. Do you have a flashlight?"

"A flashlight, are you kidding? I didn't even bring a phone. You're the Girl Scout, Luci."

"Well, there was never a badge for two old ladies stuck in the woods alone. And I can't see the benefit of starting a fire and toasting marshmallows."

Suddenly the breeze picked up. Luci's eyes darted to the right. "Did you hear that Alyce? It sounded like a car," Luci said nervously. "But" she went on, "we haven't called them yet, Alyce. How are you at self-defense? What could we use as a weapon?"

"A woman I worked with said to grasp your keys, put the part that goes into the ignition sticking out through your middle finger and index fingers, and aim for his eyes."

"Fabulous idea Alyce, but we didn't drive and we don't have keys. At least we have leftovers from the tea if we're stranded for a long time," Luci added encouragingly.

"I'm starting to get thirsty," Alyce lamented. "I think we can call home now. It's been fifteen minutes. They should be home from the station by now."

"Okay, Alyce." As she picked through her cavernous bag for her phone, Luci hesitated. "How are we going to explain this? Maybe we can say the lady next to us was coughing so loudly, we didn't hear the conductor announce the Hanson Station."

Alyce shook her head in disbelief. "That's not going to fly."

Nodding in agreement, Luci said, "You're right. They *will* certainly believe that we were talking so much planning our next adventure, we didn't realize that this would turn into its own adventure." But when Luci dialed home, the phone continued to ring. "I don't get it, Alyce. Why hasn't it gone to the answering machine?"

"Why don't I call my house and see if Ron is home?"

Meanwhile, in Hanson, their husbands expected a message would be waiting for them at home. When Jim didn't have a message waiting, he called Ron. "Nothing here either," said Ron. "We'll have to wait to hear from one of them. Whoever gets the message will pick them up."

Luckily for these damsels, Ron was just hanging up when Alyce called.

"Hello, Ron," said Alyce sheepishly, "We're so sorry we missed our stop."

"What happened?"

"We were so engrossed in our conversation we never heard the announcement."

"What could be so engrossing after you spent the day together that you could not hear the loudspeaker? Did many passengers leaving give you a hint?"

"Just come and get us. We're at Halifax Station."

"Where is that?"

"I don't know. It's somewhere in Halifax. It's dark and scary here. Drive around Halifax and when you see train tracks, drive in."

Alyce turned to Luci and said confidently, "Ron is on his way."

"No problem, Ron has an excellent sense of direction. I hope he comes quickly. Standing in these heels is getting uncomfortable," said Luci.

After more agonizing minutes, they decided to walk toward the main road a quarter mile away. Halfway there they saw two very welcome headlights approach, and they were rescued.

As she got into the car, Alyce gave Ron a quick kiss and presented her peace offering. "We brought you some pastries from high tea." Thankfully, Ron was very understanding. Of course, over the many years of experiencing their crazy antics, he's learned patience.

High tea continued through the years. The Mandarin had an Asian decor but maintained the traditional preparations for high tea. The elegant chocolate fountain with fresh fruit was a highlight. The Jonathan Snow House served tea outside on the veranda, which gave it an old-world Southern charm. The Langham was also lovely and put its individual spin on high tea. Other venues included the Plymouth Tea House and a lovely little tea store in Mashpee Commons that was casual, cozy, and offered different tea-related items in addition to serving high tea.

While visiting Alyce and Ron in Florida, Alyce took Jim and Luci to visit the Flagler Estate. It was a lovely March day in Florida as they toured the Gilded Age museum. Full access to the museum allowed its beauty to shine. Then they noticed that they also served high tea. The gals couldn't resist that. Luckily, they arrived before the tea service stopped at 3:00 p.m.

Tea was served in the Cafe des Beaux-Art, a large room flooded with light from the glass ceiling and surrounding Palladian windows. The waiter led them to an oversized, linen-covered table set with silver and the Whitehall Collection china from the museum. Each table was decorated with a single amaryllis in a bulb-shaped pewter vase. At this late hour, they were the only ones there. A congenial waiter gave them the royal treatment with more food than was customary, including delicious French macarons. It was definitely a Gilded Age high tea delight.

CHAPTER 26

Touring Houses and Museums

The Junior League of Boston Designer Showhouse

For a few years, Luci and Alyce visited the Designer Show House, customarily held in the spring. The houses were magnificent estates in Newton and Boston. Designers from all over the state donated their time and materials to decorate a particular room or outdoor area. The money raised from their efforts would help women and at-risk girls of the Boston area.

The tour itself was never disappointing. The designers competed for first, second, and third place honors. The rooms were inspirational rather than practical because the wallpapers and furnishings probably cost more in each room than the ladies had originally paid for their houses.

But the tours gave these quasi-amateur decorators insight into patterns, colors, and trends. For example, one year they noticed the emergence of stenciling. Their homes that spring were abloom with stenciled walls. Then they noticed the designers relying less on wallpaper and more on faux painting. That spring, they learned how to sponge paint walls.

Designers were also highlighting beautiful wood floors instead of wall-to-wall carpets throughout the house. Since their houses were built in the late 60s and early 70s, all their rooms had wood floors that had been overlaid with carpets. Off came the carpets to reveal gleaming unscratched floors. To these dreamers' delight, each experience was meaningful, and they looked forward for many years to visiting the designer houses.

Christmas House Tours

Although these wannabe designers were always on the lookout for inspirational house tours, they were especially active hunters around the holidays. Three of the more popular places they visited were the Daniel Webster House in Marshfield, the Vanderbilt Mansion in Newport, and house tours in Bristol, Rhode Island, which included Blithewold Mansion.

The Daniel Webster House in Marshfield was a perfect choice because its location made it less susceptible to the vicissitudes of Mother Nature, in contrast to the other two sites that often required driving an hour on snow-covered highways. Every year, designers were each given a room to decorate while maintaining an overall color scheme. This mansion became one of Luci's favorites because the house's size qualified it as a mansion, but it wasn't so large that it would require running shoes to get from one room to another. In essence, one could imagine a family actually living there.

She pictured herself entering through the high double doors to the vestibule, placing her keys on the ornate credenza, and checking herself in the gold-edged mirror. Ahead of her was the beautiful, oversized fireplace with the gilt-edged portrait of Daniel Webster reinforcing the pedigree of the house. Balancing the formality of the portrait was the mantel, beautifully decorated with wire-edged ribbon bows, sparkling ornaments, and tiny lights casting shadows across the room.

To the right was the formal living room. Several large, full-height windows flooded the room with afternoon light. Velvet swags and jabots adorned the windows, and matching velvet sofas highlighted the room's elegance. The decorating theme was nature. The living room tree was filled with birds, pinecones, fresh cranberry garlands, and other natural elements. Another fireplace to the right was topped by a white ceramic deer display and centered with a pineapple, a symbol of hospitality.

Next to the living room was the dining room with yet another fireplace and a built-in cupboard filled with the family china. The large dining room was set for a grand holiday feast. How easy it was to envision her family sitting around the table, glasses raised.

But even more impressive for Luci was the butler's pantry. Glass-doored cabinets filled with china, crystal, and silver serving pieces lined the room. For someone who hadn't met a cooking or baking implement that she didn't like, it was like entering Santa's workshop. Alyce quickly interrupted Luci's reverie so they could continue the tour.

A magnificent staircase led to the second floor. As they ascended the ornate and winding staircase, they admired the palladium windows on the first landing. On the second level they marveled that the early settlers must have been much shorter in stature, because the beds were smaller, lower, and appeared far less comfortable, especially because ropes served as the structure for the feather mattress.

One walk-in closet held period clothes, including a child's delicate christening outfit. A small area between bedrooms was filled with children's toys. Two bathrooms completed the upstairs. In one bathroom the tub was filled with clear glass balls to resemble bubbles.

The kitchen itself had been modernized, but was replete with gingerbread houses and a glass-door cabinet with tiny white lights and ornaments interspersed among the crystal glassware. A fresh pine wreath adorned the fireplace.

They ended their tour in the gift shop where hot cider and cookies were served. This delightful tour really put them in the spirit of the season.

Much grander in size, the Vanderbilt Mansion in Newport made the Daniel Webster's look like a carriage house, but the trip to Newport was always special because of the many mansions and quaint shops. The hour-long car ride gave the gals time to chat and to plan their holiday activities. Of course, the house was magnificent in all its gilt-edged finery.

One year the dominant decorating color was red, and there were more poinsettias in the house than they had ever seen. The natural architecture alone was reason to visit, and the sheer proportion of the rooms and the quality of the furnishings would make the visit memorable. In fact, to some extent, too much holiday flavor would obscure the natural beauty of the mansion.

Indeed, the trustees must have come to the same conclusion because a few trees and poinsettias were the major decorations. Although the visitors didn't find holiday decorations to replicate, they thoroughly admired the workmanship and the utter grandiose excess of this Gilded Age Grande Dame.

The Christmas Tour of Homes in Bristol, Rhode Island, was especially enjoyable for Luci because her family home was there, and most of her family still called Bristol home. One of the advantages of attending this tour was that they met at her sister Linda's house and started the tour with hors d'oeuvres and wine. A bonus was that Linda always decorated her house so beautifully that it was like having an extra house to tour. While the urge to continue consuming Linda's delicious appetizers was pressing, they soon realized they had more houses to visit.

The tour included several well-appointed private homes. Two mansions were also included: Lyndon Place, a summer mansion owned by the Colts and Barrymores, and Blithewold, a mansion on the edge of town originally owned by the Van Wickles. These mansions of the Gilded Age offered visitors a glimpse of life for these magnates in a time before income tax.

The houses were all unique. One house had a massive Dickens house display that must have taken weeks to set up. Another house had an angel theme. Every conceivable place was occupied with angels of various shapes and sizes. One house was like Candy Land, where candy canes, jars of candies, and gum drop trees filled the space. Another house showcased the owner's floral abilities with wreaths and flower arrangement artfully displayed. The final house was on the water, and although they had minimal decorations, the view alone was worth the visit.

Because Linda lived in Bristol, Luci and Alyce got inside information about the houses and their occupants, including one house that they admired for the sheer vastness of the decorations that enveloped the entire place. Linda said that the owner started decorating the day after Thanksgiving.

Blithewold is a beautiful mansion whose lovely grounds can't be fully appreciated on a crisp winter late afternoon. But if you visited in the summer, you could look out the living room window toward the garden and see the sweeping vista of Narragansett Bay. In fact, the view could be captured from the sofa on the opposite side by looking at the large mirror placed for optimum views.

As you entered the mansion, a floor-to-ceiling decorated tree set the Christmas tone. Sauntering through the rooms was a delight. Although the decorations were simple and elegant, the house itself shone. Not as large as the Vanderbilt mansion but larger and grander than the Daniel Webster, Blithewold showed the elegance of a time when industrial titans had the capital to build summer homes that were beyond the dreams of the average person.

They saved Lyndon Place for last. It, too, was a summer mansion and had the period detail of the era. The dining room was fully decorated for an elaborate holiday dinner with a myriad of forks, spoons, and glassware to challenge today's more modest diner. One of the most interesting features was the round staircase. Standing on the main floor, one could look upward to the fourth floor, a winding architectural feat. When their tour was over, they headed for the carriage house, with its beautiful stone facade, for refreshments.

A buffet table was set up with a generous assortment of goodies and large silver urns with coffee—both regular and decaffeinated—tea, and hot cider. Dining tables were set for people to relax, enjoy their refreshments, and imagine being guests when one of the original owners held their summer parties. The ladies imagined an orchestra playing softly in the background, the guests in long, sweeping summer dresses, hair upswept in elaborate plaits with pearls adorning their necks. How easily they could imagine themselves in this Downton Abbey-like setting.

By the time the tour was finished, the sun had set, and it was time to return home to reality. As usual, the ride home was an animated one as they had much to discuss.

Museum Musings

Many Tuesday get-togethers included trips to museums. Those trips were quests for knowledge of history, places, and cultures. The key to enjoying their visits was to plan ahead and research some of the artists or artifacts that they would be viewing. Whenever one of them read about an upcoming exhibit that would appeal to them, off they went.

One of the most popular Boston museums they visited was the Fine Arts Museum. They have returned a few times wandering through the museum admiring the magnificent paintings and artifacts. The Fine Arts Museum's Egyptian collection is especially worth seeing with its extensive display of Egyptian mummies and sarcophagi.

In 2011 the ladies had an opportunity to view the exhibit created by Dale Chihuly, the glass artist. The display included enormous structures of glass stretched into intricate designs and producing spectacular colors. The display had arrived in seven hundred and seventy-five boxes filled with thousands of pieces that were then assembled onsite.

Isabella Stewart Gardner Museum was enjoyed by our two kindred spirits many times. Modeled after a Venetian Palazzo, the museum is unlike many others. The courtyard is visible from any gallery in the museum. All the figures in the courtyard are female. The living collections of plants that change almost every month set the stage for a lovely place to sit and enjoy the beautiful surroundings.

The first time the ladies went, they were a bit overwhelmed, but the next time, they rented the earphones for the audio guided tour, which really enhanced their experience. One time they bought box lunches at the restaurant and sat on the courtyard edge, basking in the beauty of the museum. Another time, they enjoyed quiche and tea in the restaurant.

Heritage Museum and Gardens in Sandwich, Massachusetts, was also memorable. On a beautiful summer day, these museum goers were transported to a new world of landscape beauty. The gardens along the trails were filled with thousands of plants, including rhododendrons, hydrangeas, daylilies, and an extensive hosta collection.

The grounds are on the banks of the Shawne Pond. To their delight they came upon a windmill surrounded by tulips and were instantly transported to Holland. One of the buildings they entered housed an exhibit of classic cars, and another had a beautiful carousel.

The museum also offered an outdoor interactive space for children to play and learn. With over a hundred acres to explore, they were determined to return for another visit. In 2015 the park added a new feature: four distinct rope course trails. Our adventurers were game for giving rope swinging a try. However, one look at the height of the ropes swinging from tree to tree, and they quickly discounted that activity. Their swinging-from-tree days were over. Safety was enjoying the flowers and landscaping from ground level.

Arriving at Louisa May Alcott's Orchard House in Concord, Massachusetts was like stepping back in time. The tour docent was very informative, giving them anecdotes of what life was like for Louisa and her sisters. The actual desk where Louisa May Alcott wrote *Little Women* was displayed in the house.

Amos Bronson Alcott, Louisa's father, was an educator and a transcendentalist, and he was very ingenious. Not wanting to go outside during the Northeast winters, he built part of the house over the outside well, resulting in the only house around with inside plumbing. The gift store was well stocked with many of Louisa May Alcott's books.

Wanting to share their adventures with their husbands now that they were all retired, Luci and Alyce planned a trip to Nantucket that included the men. A boat trip on the Steamship Authority's high-speed ferry brought them to Nantucket in about an hour. The boat ride, sightseeing, and lunch with their two favorite men made for a lovely summer day. Oh, the joys of retirement.

Once on land, they meandered over the cobblestone streets past the little boutiques and came upon the whaling museum. They were hooked. This was a definite stop. Ron, the beach and sun worshiper in the group, opted out and decided to enjoy the sun and sea while the others explored the museum. The Hadwen and Barney Oil Factory was part of the museum and played a big part in the economy of Nantucket during the booming whaling years. They saw a two-story post and beam-level press, the only one still in existence in the world.

The documentary film of the sinking of the *Essex*, a Nantucket Whaling Ship, was both entertaining and educational. The *Essex* was struck by a sperm whale in 1820 in the middle of the Pacific Ocean, thirteen hundred miles from shore. The story of the *Essex* was believed to be the inspiration for Melville's *The Tale of Moby Dick*.

After the tour, they reunited with Ron, who announced he had broken one of his flip-flops, causing an uneasy gait that led to blisters. Off Alyce and Luci went to find comfortable flip-flops for Ron while the men waited on the bench. A lovely seafood lunch and a glass of wine on the cruise back to the mainland completed the trip and made for a wonderful excursion.

Rotch-Jones-Duff House and Garden Museum, in New Bedford, Massachusetts, was a stately Greek revival mansion built by William Rotch Jr., a whaling merchant, in 1834. The house has been occupied by three families: the Rotch family beginning in 1834, the Jones family in 1851, and the Duff family from 1935 until 1981. The spacious property occupied a whole city block. The beautiful landscape included a gazebo and multiple gardens filled with heirloom roses.

The ladies reflected on how these families enjoyed an affluent life of tea on the porch, afternoon garden parties, and holiday balls. At the end of the tour, they were given a small glass dish as a souvenir. Energized by the fresh air and beautiful grounds, they walked to the Black Whale, a seafood restaurant on the waterfront a few blocks away. The ambiance was lovely and the food delicious, a perfect way to top off another delightful day.

The Otis House Museum, in Boston, Massachusetts, was a Federal Era design built in 1796 by the renowned architect Charles Bulfinch, a friend of Harrison Gray Otis. The family lived and entertained lavishly in this elegant house. When guided through the different rooms, visitors can view some of the elaborate furnishings and even some of the period clothing still hanging in the closets.

Yellow, thought to aid in the digestive process, was a logical choice for the dining room. The yellow theme continued in Sally Foster Otis's bedroom, with a beautiful canopy bed and yellow tapestry drapes. Perhaps she had a penchant for eating in bed. Or perhaps yellow was selected because originally the rooms had no lighting fixtures and were lit only by candlelight, and thus yellow added light to the room.

In the beautiful brick-walled kitchen, multiple stoves, sinks, and utensils of the period dramatically revealed that many servants were an integral part of preparing meals for the family. The butler's pantry, with its displayed sets of china and crystal stemware, gave these visitors a glimpse of the opulence only reserved for the very rich.

The proximity to Plymouth, Massachusetts, for our museum hoppers, made it a natural destination to absorb the history in "America's hometown." However, visiting "the Rock," as the 1620 Pilgrim landing site is affectionately called, was anticlimactic.

Visitors approach what appears to be a Roman gazebo protected by a wrought iron fence. The Dedham granite stone, or what some might describe as a boulder, is believed to have been deposited by glacial activity about 20,000 years ago. Though the authenticity of the rock as the Pilgrims' first step on American soil may be questioned, it remains a symbolic representation of the Pilgrims' arrival on American shores.

For Alyce and Luci, a more significant historical experience was visiting the National Monument of the Founding Fathers. The monument faces the direction of Plymouth, England. Standing eighty-one feet high, this granite monument is dedicated to the hundred and two passengers aboard the *Mayflower*.

Five granite figures represent the pilgrims' guiding principles: Faith, Morality, Law, Education, and Liberty. The central and tallest figure representing Faith is a female holding a bible. Surrounding and below the faith figure are the four additional figures: a female figure holding the Ten Commandments representing Morality, a sitting male figure representing Law, a seated female figure representing Education, and a sitting male warrior representing Liberty. Our two visitors found a certain irony between the monument's title "Founding Fathers" and the predominant female representation of their guiding principles.

Luckily for these two women, their arrival coincided with a bus tour. The tour guide, dressed in period garb, emerged from the bus and escorted his visitors to the monument. He set the stage by first describing the harsh conditions the pilgrims endured on their voyage. Remaining in character throughout the presentation, the guide proceeded to explain the history and meaning of the statue. Both Luci and Alyce thoroughly enjoyed the presentation.

Another visit included the Mayflower Society House Museum in Plymouth, Massachusetts, an eighteenth-century home and formal garden that overlooks Plymouth Rock and the harbor. In modern times the view has been partially obscured with development, but when the house was built, the unobstructed ocean views must have been breathtaking.

Edward Winslow, a loyalist who would eventually flee to Nova Scotia, leaving behind his properties, was the original owner. In 1775 his grandson, another Edward Winslow, added to the four-room house, resulting in this grand mansion. Over the next three centuries many influential Plymouth families called the Mayflower House home. The Mayflower Society Museum is also located in the house and is replete with historical artifacts and documents.

The house itself is furnished in the style of the period. Sitting in one of the rockers on the Mayflower front porch gazing at Plymouth Bay and the Atlantic beyond is a lovely way to enjoy Plymouth on a sunny afternoon. The back of the house also holds a treasure. Entering through a trellised arbor, visitors enjoy the visual delight of a garden with a varied array of blooming perennials. Meandering through its artfully arranged flower beds in spring and summer is especially lovely and serene.

CHAPTER 27

Making Merry in Magog

In 2001 Jim and Luci bought a cottage in Quebec, Canada, in a little town called East Bolton. The cottage, surrounded by mountains, had one hundred and eighty feet of frontage on Lac Long, an ecological glacial lake. Quebec is the only Canadian Provence to use French as the dominant language, which enhanced their love of the area, its people, and its culture.

With only Luci's high school French, conversations were limited at first, but Luci found that once you tried to speak French, most people responded in English. Luckily for the Records, their neighbors were bilingual, with English being their dominant language.

They were anxious to share this experience with family and friends. It didn't take long to discover that this two-bedroom, one-bath cottage did not easily accommodate their children and grandchildren en masse. They began what Luci called "a little renovation." They would raise the roof and create more space upstairs.

In 2004 they began the project. Luci was still working, so Jim was relegated to supervising the renovation. It turned out to be a bigger project than they had expected, so they did Phase One—building the outside structure—and reserved Phase Two for finishing the inside.

By now Luci's mother, affectionately called Big Vovo, was living with them in Hanson, and Luci decided to bring her to Canada. Jim, already retired, was able to get to Canada earlier in the week, so Luci had to drive her mother by herself. Because she had to wait until school was over for the day, they got a late start.

Luci's mom was not a shrinking violet and had maintained her maternal right to treat Luci as she had when Luci was a young girl. Big Vovo never diverged from the hierarchy that designated her the boss, even though Luci was a responsible adult. Big Vovo also felt responsible to alert Luci to all vehicles on the road that might impede her success as a driver. Her unspoken sighs and gasps signaled her copilot status.

Finally, they were out of Boston and the signaling slowed down. As they proceeded north, they left the hustle and traffic of the city and trees replaced skyscrapers. Big Vovo loved the mountain scenery and wistfully observed, "So many trees. I wonder who planted all these trees."

Unfortunately, as the sun went down and the mountain roads became curvy, the trees took on a more ominous look. The last hour was torturous. The signaling moans and "be careful on that turn" grew in volume and quantity. At last, they made it to the cottage, but it was too dark to really see the beauty of the water.

Big Vovo was eager to rest, recounting to Jim the dangers of the trip and how fast Luci drove around those curves. "I thought we were going to fall off the mountain," she cried. Jim nodded in sympathy and quickly made up the sofa bed.

The next morning, Big Vovo was up bright and early and sitting on the porch with her crochet, marveling at the glistening water and the sound of the loons.

When one of the upstairs bedrooms was partially completed, Luci and Jim wanted to share the cottage experience with Ron and Alyce. When Luci mentioned that Ron and Alyce would be coming over the weekend, Big Vovo remarked, "Oh, a strange man. I'm not comfortable being in the house with a strange man." Luci convinced her that Alyce would be with that "strange man" and that she would be safe.

Big Vovo loved Alyce, but she was always a bit jealous of the time Luci spent with her. Every Tuesday, she would turn to Jim and huff, "Hmmm, it's Tuesday, Alyce's Day." Even after Alyce became a snowbird, Big Vovo would alert Jim in May, "Alyce will be back soon. That's the last we'll see of Luci."

Meanwhile, Alyce was excited to visit Luci and see the cottage. This would be the first visit either Ron or Alyce had made to Canada. Because this was before one needed a passport to travel there, their guests enjoyed the ride up and easily crossed the border. Alyce was driving as they entered Canada, and after passing through customs, Ron noticed the speed limit was 110. "Wow," our Mario Andretti remarked, "I'm going for that, Ron." She slowly accelerated and off they flew down the highway.

When they reached their exit, the speed limit changed to 50, so they now had to slow it down a bit. However, this seemed a bit dangerous even to our racer, for the roads were narrow and winding heading into Magog. They now were chugging along at a much safer clip and arrived at the cottage.

Jim and Luci greeted them at the door with hugs and kisses. They enlightened them that the metric system was the preferred weight and measurement system in Canada and when they were going 110 mph, they should have been going 66 mph. On those narrow streets, 50 mph should have been 25 mph. Everyone was relieved that Alyce hadn't been stopped for reckless driving by the Mounties. A close call indeed.

Before the end of the weekend, Ron had charmed Big Vovo and he lost his "strange man" status. Since Big Vovo was happiest sitting near the dock crocheting, with the afghan over her legs despite the summer weather, the foursome was able to go off on their own. Luci and Alyce went to Spa Eastman, a sprawling health facility located about five minutes from the cottage. The spa was calming, serene, and totally relaxing.

While the ladies had facials, Jim took Ron to visit the local goat farm for some fantastic goat cheese and to meet the colorful self-sufficient owner. Living in a house he built himself, the goat farmer, his wife and children, and his eighty-eight-year-old father tended the farm and vegetable garden. He had cut an opening in the bottom of his cellar and caught fish from the spring running underneath his house. The farm family drank goat milk, made goat cheese, and primarily lived off the land.

Later, the foursome went to the park in Magog, about fifteen minutes away, to grab something to eat and people-watch, especially the roller bladers who put on quite a performance. No trip to Magog would be complete until Jim showed Ron the local barber shop, which replicated a nineteenth-century barbershop. Also noteworthy, according to Jim, was that he had seen Donald Sutherland, a Canadian, on one of his trips. Mr. Sutherland's home was in the area, and he was often seen there. It was a lovely weekend, and during the trip back home, Alyce observed the real speed limits.

They returned a couple of years later. Again, the ladies went to the spa. The weather was beautiful, so Ron and Alyce could take advantage of the lake. They used the paddleboat and Alyce kayaked. This time, Luci and Jim took them to Knowlton, a quaint old English Royalist town about twenty minutes away. Luci had heard they had a theater and thought that would be a fun activity. Wrong. The production was very avant-garde and completely bored the men.

One thing that *was* successful was a trip to Dora's. One of the benefits of being in a culturally French province is the availability of good bread and French pastry. Even the markets are replete with fantastic breads and mouth-watering pastries. Because Ron likes French crullers, Jim and he went to Dora's bakery in Eastman to buy crullers for breakfast. A dozen crullers left the bakery, but only six made it to the cottage. Those crullers banished all thought of the disastrous play night.

The next morning, these health-conscious female warriors wanted to balance the cruller indulgences with a walk.

"Perfect," agreed Luci, and off they went.

While Alyce has a reasonable sense of direction, Luci has none. For Luci, GPS was a godsend. At the time, however, they neither had GPS, iPhones, nor any sense of time. They easily got lost. Somehow, they managed to continue talking and walking.

Two hours later, they found the main road on their "short walk." They weren't even in East Bolton anymore. Meanwhile, at the cottage, Ron began to worry, so he set out to look for them. Lucky for these walkers, he did find them. They were tired but very glad to see him.

Another year, the ladies were continuing their "Health Nut phase" when Luci mentioned that a friend from school took her daughter to the Canyon Spa. "Can you imagine? That cost thousands."

Suddenly a light bulb appeared above Luci's head. "Hey, we could do that in Canada. We could have a health and beauty reboot, plan only healthy meals, exercise throughout the weekend, and indulge in more than one spa activity."

"Count me in," said Alyce. Before long, they were making freezer meals for Jim and Ron, letting the children know that the dads would need company, and making spa reservations. What a weekend it was. Because they chose more than one spa activity, they had access to all the spa offerings, including the pool. The whole day was one indulgent activity after another followed by carefully prepared healthy meals and lots of exercise. Before they knew it, the weekend was over.

Steve had given Luci a tape of the *Prairie Home Companion* show, and they planned to listen to that on the way home. The show was about a fictitious hometown of Lake Wobegon "the little town that time forgot, and the decades cannot improve ... where all the women are strong, all the men are good looking, and all the children are above average." Garrison Keillor hosted the radio show, which aired in Minnesota. The hokey accounts of life in Lake Wobegon and the outrageous characters resulted in uproarious laughter from the two women. They laughed so much that Luci, who was driving, thought she would have to stop on the side of the road to collect herself and wipe away the tears that were streaming down her cheeks.

Neither woman had laughed so hard. Each story was funnier than the other. What a special night that was. They didn't want it to end. In fact, they didn't immediately go home. They realized all that laughter made them hungry, so they stopped at Friendly's in Hanover for English muffins before returning home.

That tape was so good that they wanted to share it with their husbands. What a disappointment. Neither Jim nor Ron found the humor in the stories. Jim occasionally smiled, but neither elicited the uncontrollable spasms of laughter that the ladies had experienced.

In 2006 Meryl Streep starred in the movie *A Prairie Home Companion*. The two fans were eager to relive that humorous ride home again and bought tickets to a weekday matinee. How disappointed they were. Neither liked the movie at all. They realized that nothing could replicate that unique combination of time, place, and circumstance on their ride home from Canada.

CHAPTER 28

Ooh La La

Alyce and Luci loved to travel. The big difference was that while Alyce found flying the most efficient way to travel, Luci's fear of flying made sailing off into the clear blue yonder a terrifying obstacle.

In 2010 a confluence of coincidences made a trip to Paris a reality. Alyce and her sister Kathy were thinking of taking a trip to Paris; meanwhile, at a family party at Luci's sister-in-law Marie's house, the conversation turned to travel and of course, the City of Lights was mentioned. Her other sister-in-law Roberta, an inveterate traveler, raved about the beauty and cultural significance of the iconic French city.

Caught up in the conversation and feeling safe that the discussion was only theoretical, Luci enthusiastically expressed her desire to go. Marie stated those chilling words, "Great, why don't we go!"

Unable to back down from her earlier enthusiastic response, Luci cheerfully feigned excitement. Unfortunately for Luci, Marie followed through on the idea and began researching a trip. When Luci told Alyce, a combined trip was planned, or rather Alyce and Marie scoured the internet for airlines, hotels, special passes to landmark sites, and thoroughly planned a fantastic itinerary to Gay Paree.

After trying to ease Luci's trepidations with a glass of wine at the airport, they departed from Logan Airport on September 7, 2010, at 9:30 p.m. The atmosphere of excitement and joy was so pronounced that even Luci's spirit was buoyed. They arrived at Charles de Gaulle Airport in Paris on September 8 at 1:05 p.m.

When they arrived at the Scribe Hotel on 1 Rue Scribe, the concierge told them the first cinematography had been shown at that hotel. Luci and Marie stayed in Room 126 and Kathy and Alyce were in Room 461. Alyce and Kathy's room faced a beautifully landscaped courtyard, while Luci and Marie's room faced the quaint street with its iconic window boxes studded with geraniums. In the lobby, floor-to-ceiling French windows opened to a courtyard. In the center was a dining area with a glass-dome roof where every window had a flower box bursting with colorful blooms.

That day at three in the afternoon, they walked to the Rue Rivoli, met their guide, and began their Paris Illumination and Dinner Cruise on the Seine River. Floodlights illuminated the Champs Elysees, the Louvre, and the Eiffel Tower. At 9:00 p.m. each night, the entire Eiffel Tower twinkles with thousands of little lights, a breathtaking sight. On their tour, they saw the Concord Square, Arc de Triumph, Trocadero, Invalides, Notre Dame Cathedral, and the Place du Chatelet.

At the conclusion of the tour, they went to a quaint French restaurant. A three-course dinner was served. Black currant kir, escargots, salmon on French tomatoes, mangos, and strawberry and raspberry sorbet were savored by all. The evening ended with a taxi ride back to the Scribe, capping a long and delightful day that began at 7 a.m. and ended at 2 a.m. Our ladies were exhausted.

After sleeping in the next day, they took the metro to the Nouveau Paris, saw the glass skyscrapers and the Arch de Fence, which is directly opposite the Arc de Triumph on the Champs Elysees. They walked to the top of the Arch de Fence, a full two hundred and seventy-four steps. Alyce thought Kathy was going to have a heart attack. "Maybe we should have taken the elevator," she thought. But Kathy was a champ, and all was well. They saw the Tomb of the Unknown Soldier and walked the plaza where they viewed drones for the first time. They feasted al fresco at a small cafe, where they enjoyed French croissants and quiche.

That evening the ladies splurged on a taxi ride to the Moulin Rouge, where they quickly lined up in the shorter of the two lines at the entrance. A sweet young French girl must have realized the ladies would not be going to a rock concert and quickly informed them that they were in the wrong line. After thanking her in both languages, they quickly changed lines.

Once inside the Moulin Rouge, they were escorted to a table close to center stage. Immediately, wine was served. They had a sumptuous dinner of lobster and scallop bisque, julienned vegetables, rack of lamb, green beans, sorbet with strawberries, and lots of wine. The show was dazzling. The cabaret-style musical extravaganza included statuesque women clad in elaborately bejeweled costumes performing the can-can.

After a taxi ride back to the hotel, they reflected on the fun-filled day of talking, walking, and laughing. Alyce, using her Fitbit, informed them that they had walked 12.18 miles that day.

Having bought the three-day Metro Pass, the ladies decided that would be their mode of transportation. Clean, well-lit, and easy to navigate, the Metro provided multilingual signs and easy access to all the museums. The Louvre and the d'Orsay Museums were on the agenda for September 10. They signed up for the Masterpiece Tour. Fitted with earphones and equipped with a tablet to use as a guide, they walked through Napoleon's apartment, viewed Leonardo da Vinci's *Mona Lisa*, and admired the statue *The Winged Victory*, which depicts the goddess Nike and the Victory of Samothrace. Nike's head and arms were missing, but her right hand was discovered in 1950 and is also displayed near the statue.

After spending several hours at the Louvre, they walked through the Tuileries Garden, which surrounds the museum, pausing in the resplendent gardens to enjoy fresh iced tea at the cafe before walking to the Musee d'Orsay. At the d'Orsay, they saw some of the works of Van Gogh, Degas, Rodin, Manet, and of course Monet. They were scheduled for a tour later that week to Giverny Gardens, where Monet painted his famous water lilies.

That evening Marie, Luci, and Alyce went to the American Dream Piano Bar for a night on the town. The lead singer sang "I'm Never Going To Dance Again" for the USA tourists.

On September 11, they boarded the metro with map in hand and headed out for another day of sightseeing. Making their way through the streets of Paris, they happened upon an air grate built into the sidewalk. The next thing they knew, they were traveling with their own "Marilyn Forever" as Luci was desperately trying to control her billowing skirt, which was being lifted up by the rushing air a la Marilyn Monroe.

They savored coffee and croissants at a sidewalk cafe along their route to Montmartre and Sacré Coeur. They searched all over for Luci's friend Sisi's favorite creperie, which served a delectable confection with Chantilly cream and chestnut filling. Alas, no success.

Place du Tertre, in the eighteenth arrondissement of Paris, is a square in the heart of Montmartre famous for its artistic culture. Dressed in their iconic berets, black pants, colorful tops, and bandanas tied around their necks, the artists set up their easels. Street performers abounded in the square, one of whom was a young girl painted gold sitting on a chair holding a water pitcher. She never moved a muscle.

After all that walking, they couldn't resist treating themselves to ice cream. Gastronomically satisfied, they hopped aboard Le Petit Train De Montmartre, a colorful miniature four-seater train that traversed the area.

Returning to the Scribe for afternoon tea was both relaxing and energizing as they chatted about their Montmartre excursion. Buoyed with new energy, they scurried upstairs to write about the day in their journals before getting ready for 6:30 p.m. Mass at Notre Dame Cathedral. On their way to the cathedral, they stopped to watch some more street performers. One of which was a unicyclist who was quite comical and a super entertainer. After Mass, they headed home for a well-deserved rest.

Thanks to Alyce and Marie's well-planned itinerary, they left Paris the next day on a one-and-a-half-hour bus tour to Monet's home and gardens in Giverny. The house was a charming French cottage with yellow and blue being the dominant colors. In the homey blue kitchen, a large black stove dominated one wall shared with a blue-tiled fireplace. Hydrangeas were set on the kitchen table, and blue and white checkered drapes dressed the windows.

In the well-appointed dining room, a glass front hutch held yellow and blue dishes. The room and furniture were painted yellow, and art and dishes hung on the wall. Another tiled fireplace graced the room as well. The dining chairs were covered in the same blue and white check fabric as the kitchen drapes. The entire large country home exuded charm.

Three gardens surrounded the home: the French garden, the country garden, and the Japanese garden. Access to the Japanese garden required passing through an underground tunnel. This was the garden that had the lily pond, the subject of his famous paintings. The garden was spectacular with its ponds, waterways, bridges, weeping willow, and its myriad of lilies.

The gardens were so serene that the ladies wanted to linger, but they had to return to their bus to continue the tour toward the Epte River a half hour away. There they had lunch at The Moulin de Fourges, a picturesque farmhouse and mill on the bank of the river.

After lunch, our ladies proceeded to their next stop: Versailles. This behemoth of a palace was crowded with tourists. They entered the gilded world of King Louis XIV, who built the palace. The last monarchs to live in the palace were Louis XVI and Marie Antoinette, both of whom perished during the French Revolution in 1789.

A Japanese Art Deco exhibit, which dominated many of the rooms, was a jarring surprise when they arrived and contrasted with the opulence of the palace. Among the sites they viewed were the grand apartment, the hall of mirrors, and the queen's apartment.

They spent some of their free time enjoying the formal gardens and the spectacular fountains. The gardens at Versailles had fallen into ruin after the revolution. In 1950 the United States donated money to the restoration project, but only one-third of the gardens were restored.

The day before they left France, the requisite souvenir shopping began. They shopped at kiosks and the famous Lafayette Place down on Rue Scribe. What fun they had shopping for berets, scarves, cookbooks, music, handbags, dresses, shirts, and jewelry. After all that shopping, they rendezvoused for pastries, tea, and hot chocolate at Angelina's, located at 226 Rue Rivoli. Because each lady had a different selection, they were able to sample many pastries.

During their entire stay at the Scribe, each morning the concierge would give them a map and explain which metro stop they needed. One morning he informed them that he was able to obtain four reservations that night for the Jules Verne restaurant atop the Eiffel Tower. All dressed for the occasion, they enjoyed a night of unforgettable views and exquisite food. Dazzled by the food presentation, they were delighted to be there.

Afterward, they walked from the Tower to their hotel. The surrounding area was filled with vendors selling small little rockets that would fire colorful lights when flown into the air. Marie and Alyce were enthralled and wanted to purchase some for the grandchildren. What a magnificent night they had on their last night in Paris. The next day the Eiffel Tower had a bomb threat and was closed to the public.

On September 14, they left the Scribe Hotel at 10:45 a.m. for the airport. After grabbing a sandwich at the airport, they boarded the plane for home. It was the end of a spectacular week. Ron met them at Logan Airport with a bouquet of flowers for each of them, a romantic gesture fitting travelers returning from the most romantic city in the world.

PART VII

The Shop 'Til You Drop Phase

CHAPTER 29

Bargain Shopping and Thrifting

While each of our ladies promoted the benefits of retail therapy as an enhancement to positive mental health, neither advocated wild spending sprees. Their mantra was that finding bargains was the only acceptable way to spend their hard-earned money. Both women were in control of household expenses, which necessitated weekly trips to keep their families fed, clothed, and their homes functioning. What better way than to shop together?

Tuesday was designated as their day to shop. At first, they would go to the malls to see what was "in." No sense in getting a bargain if you got something that was a passing fad. Classic, comfortable, and durable were their requirements. They rummaged through sale racks with keen eyes and an even keener sense of value. Both seamstresses, they could spot shoddy workmanship at a glance.

When department store prices were too high, they became patrons of Marshalls and T.J. Maxx, especially their sale racks. Then they discovered the Talbot's outlet in Hingham. Though some may find the clothing a bit dowdy, it was well made and lasted. They never went out of style, especially when the gals became "women of a certain age," and were freed from the slavery of fashion. Their daughters, however, always seemed to wrangle them into fashion's latest trends.

They discovered that Twice as Nice in Pembroke had a nice selection of pocketbooks. Twice as Nice also provided the ladies with exercise because to reach it involved climbing a mountain of stairs, an easy task for Alyce, the runner, and an exercise activity for Luci.

For sewing material, Luci took Alyce to a factory in Pawtucket, Rhode Island, that had made cloth for Martha Stewart and other important fabric lines. At the time, they were selling 108″-wide fabric. That was perfect for Luci to make a comforter, bed skirt, and shams with Martha Steward material for $2.50 a yard. It was a super bargain day. Alyce made shades for her sister Kathy's TV room. Years later, Luci made a queen sheet set with her material. Alas, that factory is no longer there, but while it was it was a wonderful resource for these seamstresses.

Another resource in Rhode Island was the ribbon factory. Many a holiday decoration was completed after a trip to the factory. In their early years, these mothers were still doing a lot of sewing and decorating, but as time passed, their sewing needs diminished and so did their trips to the outlets. Recently, they returned to the ribbon outlet to discover that prices had gone up and the selection had gone down. But they managed to squeeze in a lovely lunch at a restaurant in Cumberland, Rhode Island.

When they were planning their trip to Paris in 2010, they discovered Savers, a thrift shop in Plymouth. Rows of labeled clothing, shoes, pocketbooks, furniture, and bric-a-brac enticed the ladies. Although it wasn't fancy, it was clean and had clothing sized and labeled resembling a department store. The prices were also much better than department stores, and they had dressing rooms. Coordinating their time, they approached their search with the precision of a field marshal.

"In thirty minutes, let's check in at the register and decide whether we need more time," suggested Alyce.

"Aye, aye, Captain," saluted Luci.

One of the only difficulties when shopping together in large open-space stores is that neither Luci nor Alyce is much taller than the racks and sometimes if one is finished considerably before the other, it is difficult to find each other. But on this shopping trip, this wasn't a problem because they were shopping in the same racks. A white sweater was perfect for an evening boat ride on the Seine, black pants could be dressed up or dressed down for trips to the Louvre or al fresco dining at a cafe, cute little sundresses were ideal for visiting Monet's house in Giverny, comfortable flats would work for walks in Montmartre, and more. They mentally went through their planned itinerary and imagined what their trip would be like.

After their packages were rung up, they were giddy as they headed for the car, almost hidden by their packages. They couldn't believe their bargains.

"Alyce, my sweater even had the tags on it," cried Luci.

"I love my pants, and they still had the dry-cleaning label on them," exclaimed Alyce. Off they went for coffee.

And then it happened. After years of dropping things off at the Salvation Army Store in Hanover, Massachusetts, Luci ventured inside and discovered a thrifter's nirvana. It wasn't long before Alyce followed. Luci developed a strategy. The key was to get there exactly at ten a.m. on Wednesdays to ensure one of the store's limited carts. Wednesdays were the preferred day because on Wednesdays all clothing was half price, except clothing tagged with the color of the week.

At that point Luci wasn't buying for her children, but for her grandchildren. What a bonanza of bargains were found by both ladies. It's amazing what some people will drop off at the store. You can find brand-new, name-brand clothing. One of the drawbacks is that the clothing is sorted by color and not size.

The novice shopper is lured at first by ridiculously low prices and buys more than needed, but eventually one becomes more circumspect and selective.

One caveat: thrifting is addictive. Once you get used to buying Ann Taylor tops for $3.99, you can never go back to paying regular department store prices. Although the real magic of thrifting is in the hunt for a bargain, it is also a perfect way to help the planet by eliminating some of the excess disposables in this world.

CHAPTER 30

Thank God for GPS

If you have been reading these stories, you already know that Luci and Alyce's similarities are evident. They even share the same weakness —a lack of navigational skills. With the technological advancement of GPS, their weakness became less noticeable. Pre-GPS they were often confused as to what road led where and whether landmarks were before or after the place they intended to go. Many odometer miles became lost miles, and they became quite adept at U-turns. To be fair, their predilection for chatting while driving may have interfered with their focus. However, that's not a defense, but rather another misdemeanor.

On more than one occasion they have been known to be completely lost while traveling. On one such trip, Luci was driving with Alyce on a quest to find Roxie's Market, a market known for its low meat prices.

Successfully maneuvering Luci's old Chevy through heavy commuter traffic that morning, they made it close to Stoughton Square without one misdirection. However, unlike Robert Frost's "two roads diverged in a wood," at Stoughton Square, five roads converged together from five different directions, a nightmare for our directionally challenged ladies. Bewildered as to which road to travel, they realized they would have to ask for help, but other cars did not recognize their predicament. Beeping horns signaled full speed ahead.

Finally, congestion necessitated a slowing of traffic, and they noticed a gentleman standing on the corner they were approaching. Quickly rolling down the window, Alyce shouted, "Do you know where Roxie's is?" Then they noticed the white cane with the red tip.

Suddenly, the car in front of them moved, leaving them no time to wait for an answer. The cacophony of horns required a decision. Alyce nervously suggested, "Quick, pick any road. We'll find it eventually." They shrugged their shoulders, shook their heads, and turned right. Only it was wrong.

However, after a couple of efforts, they made it to Roxie's and filled the cooler in the trunk with meat bargains. On the ride home, they figuratively patted themselves on the back for snatching all those bargains, clearly dismissing the money burned on gas. That night very expensive pork chops were served at their houses.

CHAPTER 31

Car Calamities

Car adventures were numerous over the years. When Luci got her first teaching job, she bought a brand new 1965 sapphire blue Chevrolet Impala sedan with automatic steering and white walls. What a beauty. When she married Jim in 1967, she acquired not only a loving husband but also a 1964 white Volvo. However, by 1971 when they moved to Katydid, both cars had seen better days. The 1964 Volvo wasn't reliable, so Jim took the Chevy to work and Luci had the Volvo.

Unfortunately, the Volvo was a stick shift and Luci couldn't drive it. The suburbs are lonely without wheels and lucky for Luci, Alyce had wheels. These intrepid gals would find excuses to meet daily, whether to share a new wall color or plan their next adventure.

Always eager to learn, they decided to take an automobile repair course in 1973 at a Hanover gas station. What a sight they were in their garage "work clothes:" jeans, sweatshirts, and baseball caps. They learned how to change tires and change the oil and filter. Lessons on car safety and basic car mechanics were also part of the course.

A little knowledge is a dangerous thing. After taking the course, Luci thought, "Why not apply my new skills to bodywork? How hard could it be?" The guinea pig would be her Chevy Impala, which ran well but had body rust. Several trips to the auto body store later and armed with mesh, compound, and other tools of the trade, she tackled the project, applying the mesh and building up the compound.

Lots of sanding and a Chevy-approved paint sample later, and surprisingly it looked good. She was so proud to have Jim take it to work. Jim was careful to park the car safely away from other cars in the Veterans Administration parking lot in Brockton. How could he face Luci if a careless car door opening damaged the new bodywork?

Alas, when he returned at 4:30 p.m., the car wasn't there. Frantically, he searched the entire lot, but finally realized the car had been stolen. Days later, the car was recovered, but it had been totally stripped of everything but the freon. The bodywork was too tempting to car thieves.

Sometimes the problems with Luci's car involved odd failures. This time it was with another Chevy. It started innocently enough with a stock pot of homemade soup from Little Vozina, Luci's grandmother. Traditionally, you never left a Sunday dinner at the Lagarto home without enough provisions to feed a small army. With three kids (without seatbelts) in the back seat, a bumpy ride, and the soup cradled on the back seat floor, it was inevitably a recipe for disaster. Not only was there less soup when they arrived at Katydid, there was quite a mess for Luci to clean up.

Well, Luci's housekeeping skills must not have transferred to the car because unbeknownst to the Records, beneath the "cleaned" carpet, a process known as oxidation was taking place. The kids never mentioned that there was a certain bounce when they got in on that side of the car until one day, Jimmy stepped in and the carpet gave way. The soup had rusted out the floor!

"Oh no," Luci cried, "That's dangerous, what should we do?"

Recognizing that they couldn't afford expensive car repairs or a new car, Jim came up with a solution. He cut a piece of plywood to fit over the hole. What these misguided parents didn't know was that the hole kept getting worse under the plywood and that Jimmy and Steve would often lift the plywood to "see the road" underneath as they were traveling. Luckily for Jim and Luci, child protective services never was appraised of their actions.

But Luci wasn't the only one who had car "situations." One day Alyce was at the Hanover Mall and a man stopped her. "Hey lady, I noticed you've got a few dents here. I can fix those dents while you're shopping. Real cheap. Just twenty-five bucks and it will look as good as new." Highly efficient and a great bargain hunter, Alyce saw this as a win-win situation. Off she went shopping. When she returned later, balancing several shopping bags, she was thrilled to see that the dents had been removed and the car looked great.

"Boy," she thought, "Ron will be so impressed." But when she reached into her bag to pay him, she didn't have any money left. Ever resourceful, she said, "Mario, follow me to my bank and I'll pay you."

Mario wasn't sure she'd take off and he'd be in a car chase, but he did follow her, and all was well. Her son-in-law Bob was at the house when she returned. Since he knew cars well, she was especially proud to show off her new, dentless car.

"Gee, I don't want to disappoint you, but it's just Bondo. It's going to dry up, crack, and fly off," he said. It did hold up for a while, so it was still a bargain.

On another shopping trip, Alyce and Luci were stopping at Joanne's Fabrics for another of their sewing projects when a man parked next to them said, "Ladies, your right front tire is flat. Do you have a spare?"

"Oh, thank you, but I'll call my husband," said Alyce. After the man left, they turned to each other and Alyce said, "We can fix it with Fix-a-flat. All we have to do is go to the hardware store across the street."

Luci protested, "You do know that we will have to cross Route Fifty-Three. That's four lanes of traffic."

"Sure."

"Okay."

The intrepid duo surveyed the scene. At the time, they were in their seventies and Luci suggested that they play the "old lady card" and the cars would stop. However, thanks to their hair salons, they didn't look like gray-haired old ladies from a distance as the cars whizzed by. The days of chivalry are long gone, and the cars didn't automatically come to a screeching halt as they started to cross.

What a harrowing experience. First one lane, then another, another, and *finally* they were across the street. They bought the Fix-a-flat and made the treacherous trek back to the car. The Fix-a-flat got them home, and they both got their "exercise" as well as an adrenaline rush.

Sometimes it wasn't the cars that caused these daring darlings problems. They met two very nice young Hanover Fire Department men one beautiful summer day while they were playing tennis across from the fire station. When Luci and Alyce play tennis, the goal is not to win the game, it's to see how many times they can keep the ball in the air. Can they volley ten times, or at least five? After about an hour of play, they returned to the car to find the keys locked in Alyce's old Acura.

Conveniently, the fire station was handy, and they jogged over. That was one time it was easy to play the "old lady card." They were a bit bedraggled. The young firemen took pity on two "forgetful" old ladies, quickly left the station, and came over to open the car.

Another time they ventured to Providence Mall to do Christmas shopping. Unfamiliarity with this shopping venue might have contributed to their problems, but they couldn't find the car. The real problem was that they are always talking to each other and when they initially parked, they continued to talk and laugh and never took any notice of where they had left the car.

After two full hours, they finally found it. Always optimistic, they saw the silver lining in this experience: they got their walking in and learned the important lesson of taking a picture of their parking spot. However, they both were upset that they had to pay a seven-percent sales tax in Rhode Island. This trip, like many of their adventures, was symbolic of their friendship. Whenever they faced obstacles, they found something positive in the experience and always managed to leave the experience still laughing.

Epilogue

When our editors asked us to include an epilogue, our immediate reaction was simultaneously to groan. How much more can we reveal about ourselves? "Just update where you are now and what you are thinking of next," they suggested. Our athletic adventures continue with the recent pursuit of pickleball. Undaunted by our early shabby attempts at the singles game, we look forward to increasing our chances of success by corralling two other friends to play a doubles game. Alyce continues to run five miles a day, while Luci continues to run to the mailbox.

On a recent trip to Tanglewood, the summer home of the Boston Symphony in Lenox, Massachusetts, we were lucky enough to pick the one day a year that holds an all-day celebration of music from the Boston Pops, the Boston Symphony, and several high school orchestras among other activities. We thoroughly enjoyed our day but were also captivated by the Berkshire Women's Chorus. Although neither of us is musically gifted, we both have entertained the idea of joining a women's chorus. Probably the only people "still laughing" would be the people auditioning us. However, it remains on our "to do" list.

Both of us plan on traveling extensively this fall and more adventures should ensue this winter when Luci travels to Florida to visit Alyce. Most importantly, we remain open to exploring whatever adventures lie ahead.

Then

Now

Acknowledgments

When we decided to publish our teatime musings, we turned to Judy Kelley, a dear friend who had recently published *Dorchester Girl* and raved about her publisher. After contacting Lisa Akoury-Ross at SDP Publishing, we found our match. Not only was Lisa the consummate professional, she was warm and nurturing to two fledgling writers who were computer challenged. Thank goodness our savvy grandsons helped us on more than one occasion. Lisa and our talented editor Cath Lauria were also understanding when life intruded on our writing schedule. They made us believe that there was an audience for our stories beyond our families. Cath's keen eye helped us bring organization to the stories and has made the book better.

Judy Kelley isn't the only Kelley we need to acknowledge. The dreaded author headshots required the photographic and computer skills of her husband Rich, whose services Judy gladly offered. While we tried unsuccessfully for hours to produce two acceptable pictures, Rich accomplished the task in less than half an hour. Additionally, he sent the pictures in the proper format to the publishers. Thank you, Rich.

We'd be remiss not to acknowledge the friendship and encouragement we received from neighbors and friends. To preserve privacy, we have changed all the names except those of our family. While we recalled our adventures, we relied on the children's memories for details of many of their stories. Some details we were hearing about for the first time.

Most importantly, we thank our husbands and children for their unwavering support and encouragement. They are the joy of our lives and the inspiration for the book.

About the Authors

Luci Record　　　　　Alyce Hennelly

Luci Record, originally from Rhode Island, and **Alyce Hennelly**, a Massachusetts native, became neighbors in Hanson in 1971 and continue to be dear friends to this day. Alyce and her husband Ron raised five children while Luci and her husband Jim raised three children in Hanson.

In 2001 the Hennellys became snowbirds and retired to Florida The snowbirds return each summer and the winter holidays. The Records remain the last original family in the development. Writing the book of their adventures together was an opportunity to reminisce about the journey of their friendship and share the wisdom and humor they have discovered in finding joy in the moment and inspiration in challenging themselves.

Still Laughing
Stories from an Extraordinary Friendship

Luci Record and Alyce Hennelly

Publisher: SDP Publishing

www.SDPPublishing.com
Contact us at: info@SDPPublishing.com

Printed in the USA
CPSIA information can be obtained
at www.ICGtesting.com
CBHW070454050624
9591CB00009B/151